SKETCHBOOKS:
THE HIDDEN ART OF DES'
ILLUSTRATORS & CREATIV

German designer Daniel Kluge says, 'A sketchbook is like a valve, a pressure release system. Instead of weighing things up in my head, I give them a place in my sketchbook. Sketches are like embryos, and as soon as they have been realized, they are born and start to live.'

New York-based illustrator Lauren Simkin Berke told me, 'My sketchbooks are the most important thing I own or produce. If there were to be a fire in my building, and I had a moment to grab one thing before running out, I would take the small suitcase of my sketchbooks from the last two years.'

A sketchbook can become a companion, for some a bible. 'The familiarity of sketching is a way of grounding myself', says Andrea Dezsö, 'It allows me to retreat from the anxiety of an unknown environment, directing my attention with purpose and clarity towards a singular object of my choosing, and I can filter out everything else. When travelling I also carry a small camera and take photographs, but drawing is something I think about. It has a different personal involvement than the time investment of taking a photo.'

After a while I was almost tempted to keep a sketchbook myself. But it's not so easy. Barcelona-based illustrator Flavio Morais says, 'For me sketchbooks are a celebration of life and a freedom to experiment... One of the most important things I seek is spontaneity, and for me travelling is one of the best ways to find it. I feel free when travelling, and that's when I really love keeping sketchbooks. Travelling is a born-again experience, like being a child, and keeping sketchbooks when travelling allows a certain amount of space to express that enthusiasm and freshness, a place for inspiration and freedom.'

As Michelangelo became more well known, before handing his sketches to his assistant he would edit which sketches to keep. Editing is not censoring, it is selecting, and hopefully offering the possibility of presenting something otherwise unseen."

TOP / Renato Alarcão
ABOVE / Peter Saville

Richard Brereton, 2009

SKETCHES ARE LIKE EMBRYOS ...
AS SOON AS THEY HAVE BEEN REALIZED,
THEY ARE BORN AND START TO LIVE

CAROLE AGAËSSE

In the 1980s Carole Agaësse studied media design and animation at Gobelins, L'Ecole de l'Image, Paris. She has exhibited throughout the world, and her work is often associated with fashion. Her visual art background led to her becoming involved in graphic design, and her clients now include international press, fashion and product designers. Her illustrations have featured in catalogues, trend books, websites and brand identities. She continues her work as a digital illustrator and she also teaches at Parsons Paris School of Art and Design.

"I started putting my ideas into sketchbooks before applying to design school, after which keeping sketchbooks became part of the educational design process. It seemed a natural way to keep track of my ideas and inspiration.

Sketchbooks help me to focus and document the external world, before methods become more structured for a final project. On paper, I can experiment and develop my compositional ideas; I can design things that don't really exist. I find that sketchbooks allow me to make changes easily and are a great way of exploring the potential of ideas.

I've been keeping my sketchbooks for a long time and they've witnessed many different periods in my life. I always have one with me, be it at work or while travelling. I always have a sketchbook in my pocket, ready for taking notes on passing opportunities.

I expect that you can see my evolution over time in my sketchbooks. These days, I'm adding simple drawings with lots of notes, impressions and comments, and sometimes highly worked images.

If I can remember a dream, the next morning I will keep a track of it in my sketchbook. It's my way of keeping a record of my internal journey, and these notes often become part of my compositional ideas.

For the most part my sketchbooks are private, a personal and intimate glimpse into my creative process."

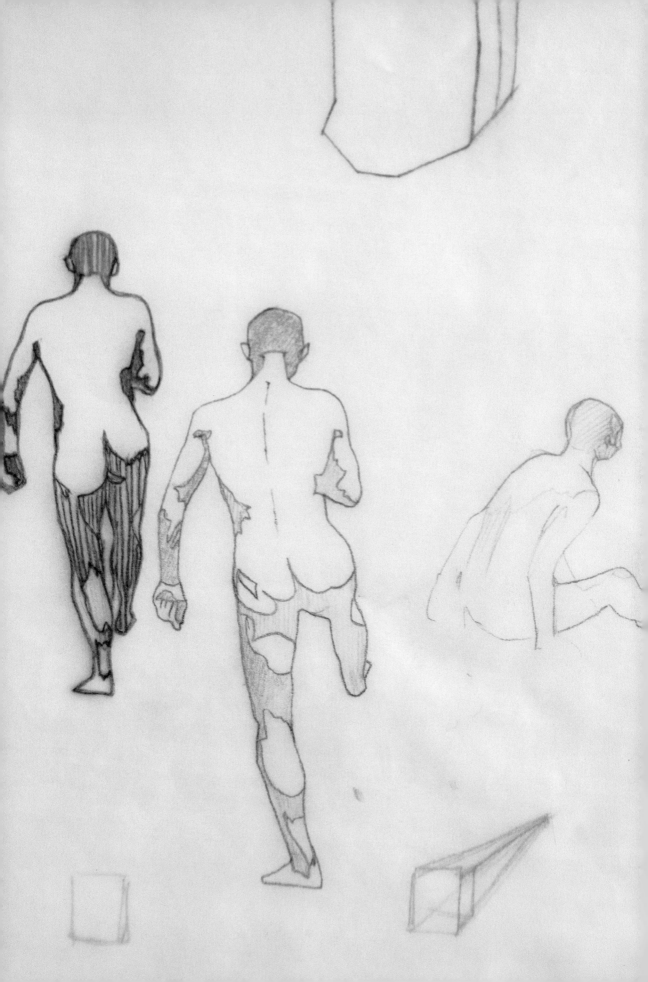

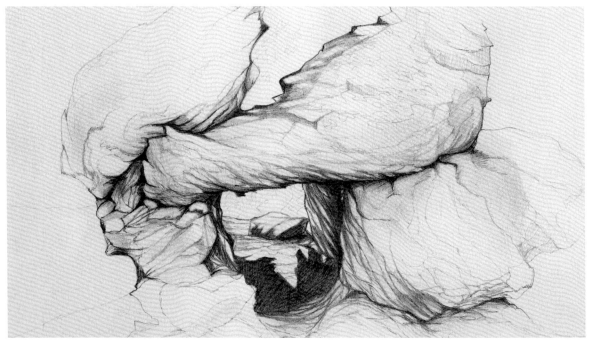

RENATO ALARCÃO

Graphic designer Renato Alarcão lives and works in Rio de Janeiro, Brazil. Educated in New York, he has been published in the New York Times, *the Brazilian newspaper* Folha de São Paulo, Playboy *magazine, and many children's books. He also runs the Estúdio Marimbondo, a small art school that runs workshops on the sketchbook (the Diário Gráfico).*

"Sketchbooks reflect what I am, my thoughts, what attracts my attention. They are a tool for keeping a temporal record of events, images and thoughts. Ultimately sketchbooks show me how I am progressing as a human being or, more modestly speaking, as an artist.

My sketchbooks keep a record of all sorts of events, trips I've taken, movies I've watched and books I've read. They're also a record of my thoughts, studies and insights, and all kinds of visual experiments that I usually don't dare to apply in my commercial work. I avoid putting anything ultra-personal or confessional in my sketchbooks. I prefer to keep these only in my mind.

I'd like to have more free time to work on a series of 'a day in the life' of sketchbooks. Some of the subjects include the people who make the costumes and floats for carnivals, the Benedictine monks from the São Bento Monastery, and the guys who work at the ferry that connects my town, Niterói, to the city of Rio de Janeiro.

The sketchbook entries I wrote when I lost my brother back in 1999 were times of bitterness, suffering and anger. They helped me to purge all those bad feelings, and I barely recognize myself in those books when I look at them today."

ABOVE / Renato Alarcão leaning against a mural at the J. Borges memorial, which celebrates Brazil's foremost north-east folk artist and printmaker

RIGHT / Detail from a spread featuring a watercolour study of a skull. "I painted this piece one day when I arrived a bit early for the watercolour classes I teach at Estúdio Marimbondo. It took me about 20 minutes to sketch this image and write a few words on the side, such as 'The opposite of life isn't death. The opposite of life is time'. I believe that the less time we have, the more intuitive the work is"

BELOW / *Sunflower and Books.* Watercolour done from life. "Setting up the elements and props for a painting is already a creative act. The old and battered envelope provided an interesting counterpart for the sunflower, glowing with life. A client wanting a mural for his restaurant found inspiration in this watercolour"

BOTTOM / *How to Draw.* Collage, drawing and watercolour. "I usually like to combine different elements at random, just to see how the visual dialogue between them develops. I rarely care about how it will look in the end, but rather enjoy the creative process of finding the right place for the right pieces"

HOW TO DRAW

BELOW / "Patricia is one of the best models I have worked with. She has been a circus artist for years and she brings all of her exciting theatrical experience into our classes. Here I sketched some students painting her"

BOTTOM / *Green Fish*. "I have a sketchbook that, ever since I flipped its very first pages, has presented a challenge: breaking the fear of the BLACK pages. The fish is a monotype taken from an old school book"

OVERLEAF / Illustration over page glued with Russian letters. "The old man is angry because his hand was stolen while he was asleep. His trousers are obviously my humble homage to Klimt's textures"

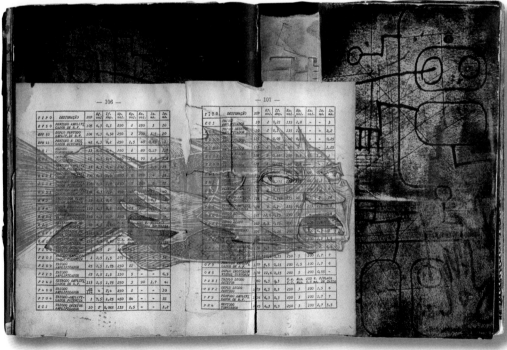

ли	си	ни	ви	мі
ле	се	не	ве	мо
лё	ся	ня	Ви	мя
лё	Си	ню	Ве	Мі
ля	Се	Ню	фи	
лю	ри	Ни	Фе	
Лю				

ле	ре	се		
ли	ря	ся		
фа	фо	фу	фы	

PABLO
AMARGO

*Award-winning freelance illustrator Pablo Amargo
(a pseudonym of Pablo Diaz Tamargo) lives and
works in Oviedo, Spain. He studied fine art at the
University of Salamanca, specialising in graphic
design and media. He works on advertising projects
and newspaper and book illustration. Clients include
Media Vaca, Editions Retz, Random House, Spain
Gourmet,* La Vanguardia *and ICEX.*

"I used to archive sketches in files, but it got to the point where I had
so many papers they began to get mixed up, so three years ago I began
keeping sketchbooks instead. Sketchbooks are a perfect way to collect
ideas and they're also a pleasure for me. Ideas often come suddenly,
and so I put them into my sketchbooks. This enables me to refer back
to them, sometimes months or even years later.

I like to work on two sketchbooks at the same time. One is for work,
with lots of little drawings, ideas for postcards and books. The second
one is for pleasure, with collages, my thoughts, people I admire, quotes
from books, news and film reviews, that sort of thing.

I like to explore ideas through drawing. For me the first idea is not
always the best one – I like to take it easy, take my time to find the right
proportions, try new perspectives, mix different drawings and so on. I
have a process whereby I use a lot of little drawings. I call them microgramas,
and I use them as the starting point for my work.

I also travel with a sketchbook, which means that I include all sorts
of additional information, such as telephone numbers and details about
places. I find I sometimes work from the travel drawings on my return.

My sketchbooks are not a removed, strange or chaotic place; they're
actually quite ordered and are a natural extension of my published work."

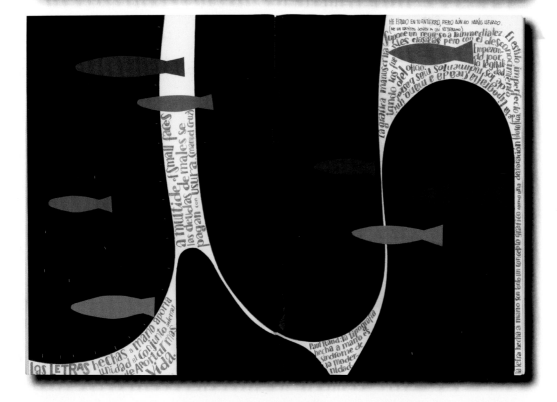

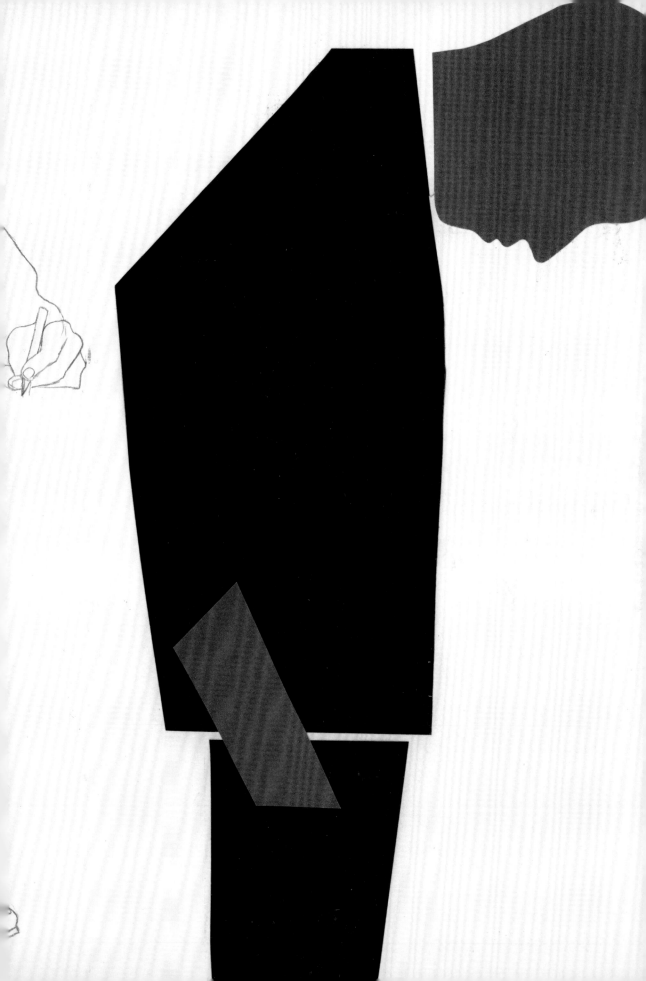

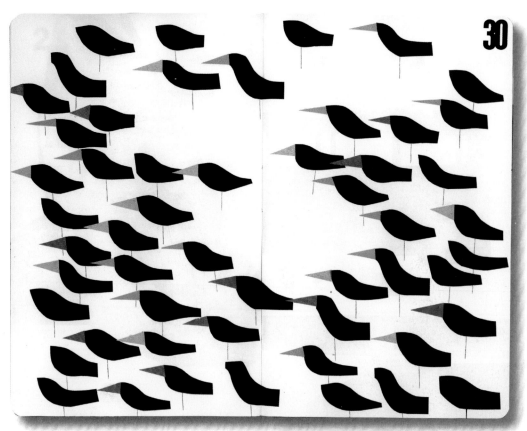

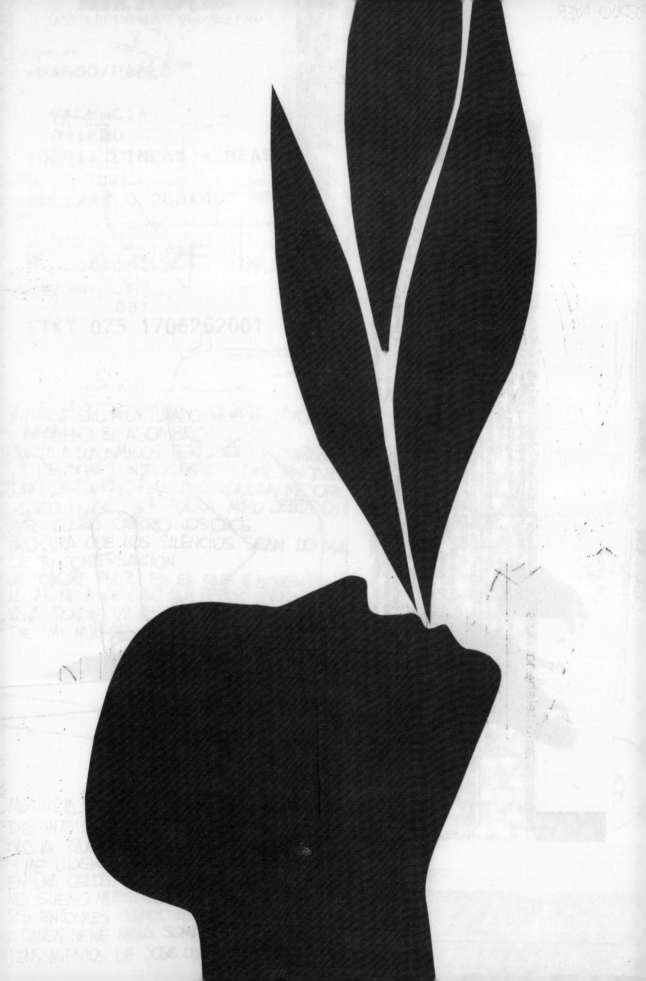

CLEMENS
BALDERMANN

Clemens Baldermann studied fine art and painting in his home town of Halle, Germany. In 1998 he moved to Munich to pursue a career in the advertising industry. After two years in the industry, during which time his work was recognized with a London International Advertising Award and by the Art Directors' Club, Germany, he decided to study graphic design. While studying he set up Purple Haze Studio, working mainly on projects for clubs and music labels, including flyers, posters and cover artworks.

"When I started in advertising, I realized that important ideas could come to you anywhere and at any time. It was then that I started regularly keeping a sketchbook in my pockets. My sketchbook is an essential tool for collecting my material and for separating the important from the unimportant. Generally I sketch everything on sheets of paper before sticking them into the sketchbook.

After reviewing my work, which might take time in some cases, I cut out or simply rip out what looks good. From time to time I stick some of my work on the wall, so that I can look over it before finally gluing it into the sketchbook. So my sketchbook is more a kind of album than a book full of scribbles. It's good training to filter things out and set them in the right context – using separate sketchbooks would stop the rotation of ideas.

There is a relationship between my work and personal life – one part won't work without the other, and my energy and my passion emerge from the contrast between the two. Anything relevant goes into my sketchbook: classic sketches, notes, stickers, photos, labels... I like collecting curious things, such as misprints and miscalculations. In the back of the sketchbook there is a wallet with a collection of snippets that I occasionally compose into collages. I like to keep everything raw. That's what a sketchbook is."

RIGHT / Magazine and photocopy snippets

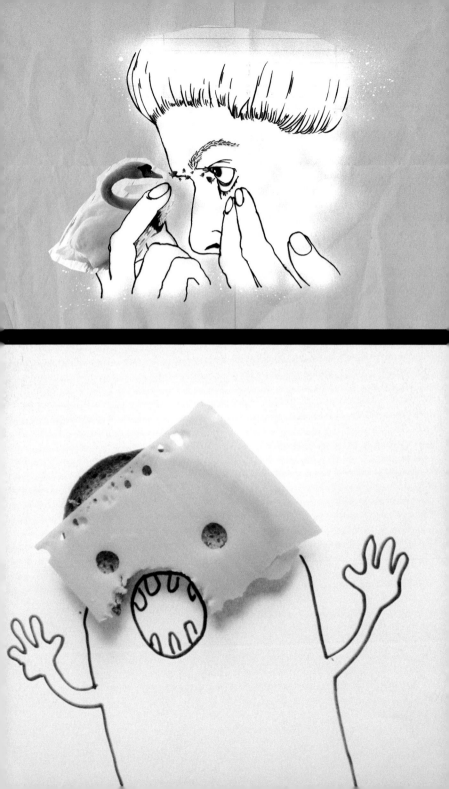

LAUREN
SIMKIN BERKE

Illustrator and painter Lauren Simkin Berke is based in Brooklyn, New York. She attended Cornell University, where she received a BA in anthropology, and the School of Visual Arts, New York, where she received an MFA in illustration as visual essay. She has had solo exhibitions at the A.I.R. and Landscape galleries in New York City and her illustration work appears in many periodicals and newspapers, including the New York Times, *the* Boston Globe *and* New York *magazine.*

"I draw every day from a different vintage snapshot, purchased from one of several flea markets or shops. The drawings are small, voyeuristic and a bit obsessive. I do them when I have my coffee in the morning. I use the line work of these drawings for my personal projects (paintings, etchings, etc.) and for my illustration work. I spend my free time seeking excellent milkshakes and cosy places to sit and read. I am currently obsessed with Roland Barthes, America's Next Top Model and Cat Power.

My first memories of having a sketchbook are at around the age of 14, though I may have started earlier than that. I was starting a new school, and spent most of my free time drawing the interior of the building as well as the park outside. I remember drawing the door to a classroom, and a tree that was outside the front doors. At that age I was just drawing everything in sight. I was drawing my teachers and classmates in class (in an attempt to stay awake), which I did in my class notebooks, not my sketchbook (owing to my teachers having very particular notebook needs).

My sketchbooks are the most important thing I own or produce. If there were to be a fire in my building, and I had a moment to grab one thing before running out, I would take the small suitcase of my sketchbooks from the last two years.

I keep all my sketchbooks, and I go through one sketchbook every six to seven weeks, which comes to seven to eight books a year.

I always travel with my current sketchbook. I'd only ever not have my sketchbook if I'm running an errand or going to a restaurant in my neighbourhood, or if I'm late and run out without my backpack (which happens all of one or two times a year).

Once I made a drawing of a cake at Billy's Bakery in NYC. It was a basic round, single-tier cake, but it was special because on top of the cake was a plastic figurine of a man in very small, tight bathing trunks. The cake was in the window as part of their decorations for NYC Pride weekend. It was pretty cute, and I was compelled to draw it as evidence (a friend once told me that I 'take a drawing' like most people 'take a photograph'). The drawing has nothing drawn around it, and no text explaining it. It's odd mostly because of the lack of explanation, and because it was drawn from life."

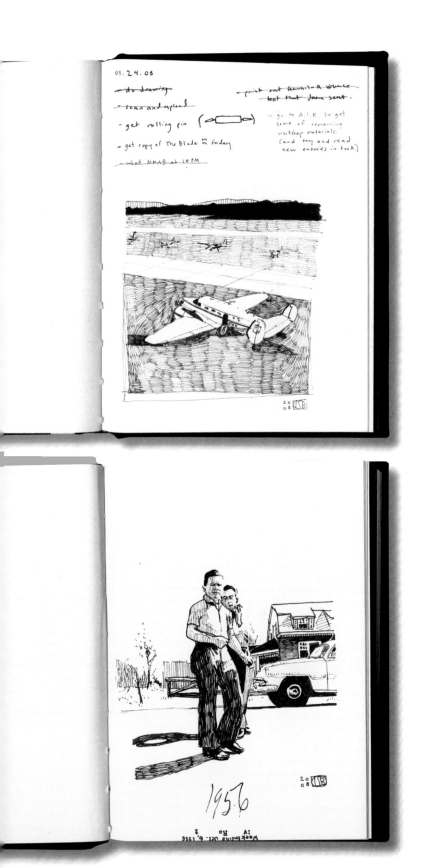

BELOW / *David,* 2006   **BOTTOM /** *Aug. 15, 1947,* 2007   **OVERLEAF /** Sketches for
The Lacy Project postcard and
Agfa-Brovlra, 2007

37

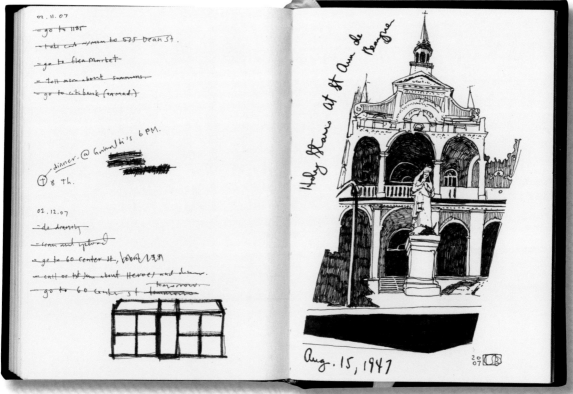

hunt J. R. Meyers pics for ref.

~~330~~

Meet w/ Teresa.

friday, early afternoon.

330 ish

~~scan recent photos, and last for drawings w/ backgrounds.~~

recent draw

2.23
3.04

do backgr

3.09
3.13

- photobooth
- contact sheet
- reg pic/snapshot

Agfa Brovira   20
                                07

An illustrator and art director from Paris, Serge Bloch recently relocated to New York. His work appears regularly in newspapers such as the New York Times, *the* Wall Street Journal, Time, Business Week, Psychologies, *the* Chicago Tribune *and* Liberation. *His work was awarded a gold medal by the Society of Illustrators' 47th Annual Exhibition in 2005. He also won the Baobab Award for Best Children's Book of the year in France in 2005 and the BolognaRagazzi Award in 2007. In 2008 an exhibition of his drawings and sketches opened at the Living with Art Gallery, Soho, New York.*

"I draw stories and write drawings. I feel that I can be expressive even with stories that have no rhyme or reason, or with sketches drawn upside down.

I like drawing for newspapers. I like newsprint. I like the grey of the text, the black of the titles, the elegance of the compositions. A page of newspaper is like a wall of a gallery where hundreds of thousands of people can visit, without being prevented by shyness from entering the gallery. You can be on a train, in bed or on a sunny bench. But that exhibit is ephemeral because, the following day, there is nothing left, just a piece of paper to dry your boots with or peel vegetables on.

I illustrate books and sometimes write them. I only do a few. My editorial work keeps me busy. I need time to let the ideas mature, but it's quick after that.

I don't always have a sketchbook on me. But when I start an ambitious project, a book for example, the solid, bound aspect of a little notebook reassures me. I know that I can throw my ideas in, and my 'black book' will keep them for me. I write and make sketches at the same time. Once the corrections are done and the project is satisfactory, I put it away. Sometimes I find an old sketchbook – it is always a pleasure to look back at it.

When I travel I sometimes take a sketchbook to take notes of my ideas. I also like to use them to play and draw with my children. Waiting periods in the restaurants or at airports are opportunities for 'drawing games'. We usually have to finish a drawing, which is a riddle. Each time I learn something new from them. Children are often artists full of genius. They are free and creative and go directly to a story.

From time to time I like to leaf through my old notebooks. I dive into my old stories again and I find ideas that I have put down and then abandoned. Sometimes one of them becomes a book project, or a drawing for a magazine or a newspaper. It is a little like a bottle of wine that has been forgotten in the cellar and has become better while ageing.

I use notebooks in an intimate way. They are my collection of ideas and shapes, a private collection."

ABOVE / Sketchbook of travel in Mexico, February 2007

RIGHT / Stamps NYC, October 2007. Research for show at the Living with Art Gallery, New York

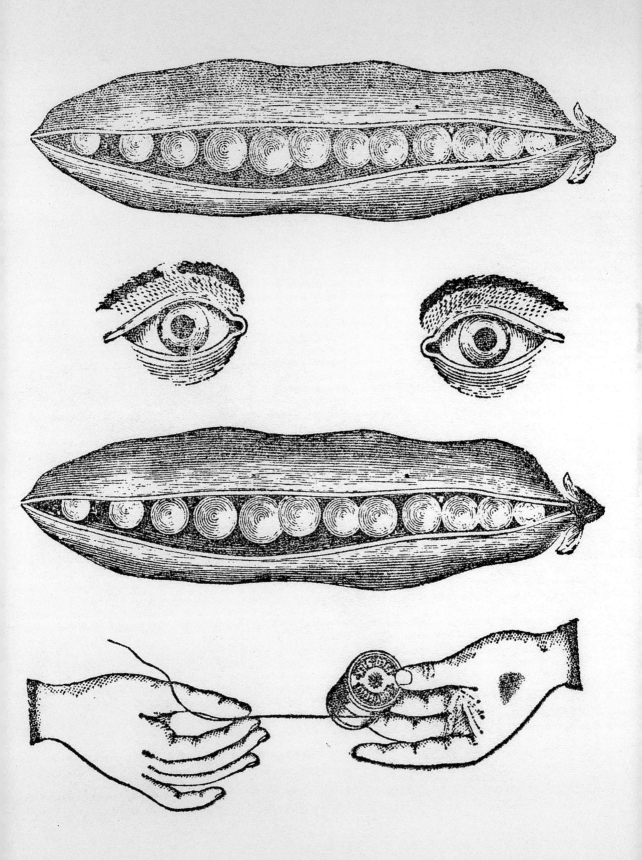

TOP ROW / "Except the bird and the sticker (found in a Paris flea market), these are sketches to find an idea for the *New York Times*' science section – subject: Why We Like Pets"

BOTTOM ROW / Elephant; Head found in an old book of anatomy; Birds for *McKinsey* magazine – subject: Modern Banks; Different papers and a small photograph of Leon

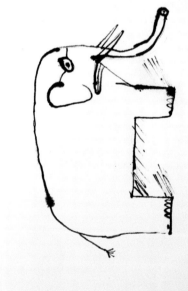

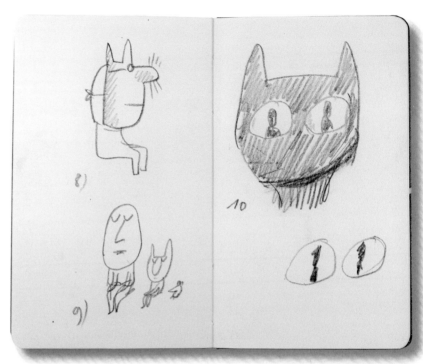

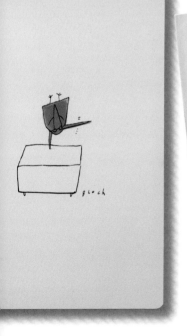

PEP
CARRIÓ

*Pep Carrió was born in Palma de Mallorca in 1963.
He is now a partner in the graphic design studio
Carrió/Sánchez/Lacasta in Madrid. He specializes
in book cover design, graphic design for brand image
and corporate communications, and exhibitions
and cultural activities. His clients include publishers,
institutions, and clothing and accessories companies,
such as Camper and Farrutx. He has also published
books in collaboration with the Spanish poet Fernando
Beltrán, with whom he has also performed several
projects:* Beat, Diving Board Poems *and* Found
Women. *In 2008 the Madrid Book Fair launched
his first book as a children's illustrator,* Una Niña
(A Child), *produced in collaboration with the Spanish
writer Grassa Toro, and published by Sinsentido.*

"It is difficult for me to remember exactly when I first started keeping
sketchbooks. Maybe the starting point was drawing in the margins of
my schoolbooks as a little boy; and, later, drawing while talking on the
telephone. I began keeping my sketches in a drawer with the idea of
compiling them afterwards into a sketchbook.

For me, a sketchbook is like a kind of a portable laboratory, a space
to mark with references, to capture the immediate, to experiment; a
memory warehouse to which I can return whenever I am searching for
an idea or when I simply want to remember an instant, a time in the past.

Since 2007 I've kept a sketchbook as a diary, where every single
day I capture an image without any particular or predetermined style.
I also keep a small sketchbook by the telephone, where I leave those
small sketches or drawings that I produce during a phone call. My third
sketchbook is devoted to compiling information and proofs of projects
that I develop later in my design studio.

My sketchbooks are open to almost everything: sketches, drawings,
photographs that I find in newspapers, texts, references, ideas, lucky
finds and discoveries – basically nothing is excluded. Some people have
suggested that they find my sketchbooks kind of disturbing or perturbing,
but I don't know why. My sketchbooks are my warehouses of memory."

ABOVE / Pep Carrió in his studio in Madrid

RIGHT / Sketchbook *Visual Diary Untitled.*
Collage, ink and gouache

OVERLEAF / Sketchbook *Visual Diary
Untitled.* Gouache

FRIDAY

August

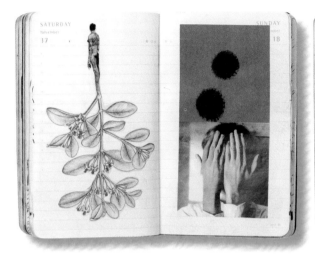

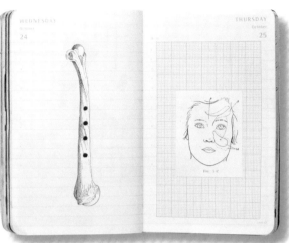

TOP ROW / Sketchbook *Visual Diary Untitled.* Black ink; Found photo and Tipp-Ex; Sketchbook *Marked Cards Chief.* Collage on card

MIDDLE ROW / Sketchbook *Marked Cards Signals.* Collage on card; Sketchbook *Marked Cards Japanese.* Collage on card

BOTTOM ROW / Sketchbook *Marked Cards Poet.* Collage on card; Sketchbook *Marked Cards Kite.* Collage on card

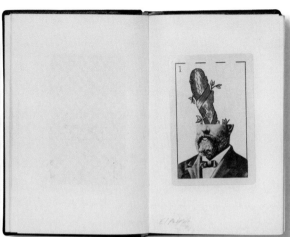

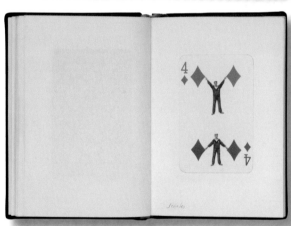

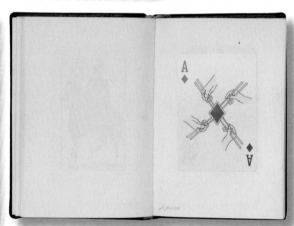

FRÉDÉRIQUE DAUBAL

Born in the south of France and later spending many years in Montreal and Amsterdam, Frédérique Daubal now lives in Paris where she works as a freelance graphic designer, art director and textile designer. She collaborates with various people and magazines, mostly on experimental ideas – Beams Japan, Blackblock/Palais de Tokyo, Bumble & Bumble, Colette, Droog, Paul Smith, Wieden+Kennedy – and on magazines including Arkitip, Graphic *and* Dutch. *Clients include Bumble & Bumble, Nike, Nokia and Sony France.*

"My sketchbooks allow me to be free, to express myself without boundaries. In a way my sketchbooks are far removed from the reality, as everything can be included and quality is not important.

When I was at college I used to transform covers, make them my own, full of drawings and notes. I liked cutting out magazine titles and pictures to make new collages.

My sketchbook is a personal compilation of such material, together with ideas and feelings, often without an end in view. Keeping sketchbooks helps me to empty my brain, while making connections between ideas without judgement. Once something is in my sketchbook I can forget about it, and then find it later. I use my sketchbooks as tools for recording my moods and thoughts. I suppose they're almost like a blog.

Secrets stay out of my sketchbooks, they don't need to be sketched. Most of the time my sketchbooks are a work in progress – ideas, lists, words, doodles, things that are important for one second and then never again, including bad drawings, things my kids say, my spontaneous reactions to things, recipes, projects, things that will never happen. I think that my sketchbook is really an open book."

cage ... ssing: 'Because Tim B... ... ... have accep... ... ...to work with him. Hon... ... ... clever... ... ...orld.' Wahlberg smiles. The ... ... and he... ... ...don, he calls: 'Hey, Tim, I've ...

BURS... ...O the screen a few months ... ... expandi... ... ...pace Odyssey, the politically ... ... released ... ... period in American histor... ... of Cold W... ... Vietnam protests and hippie ... served up p... ... ...bits of social realism along with ... ...also burst throug... ...be 20th Century Fox's biggest hit ... ...ssing $28 million (c... ...ion budget). Four sequels of d... ...owen as well as two ... ...y series and a horde of ancillary ... ...y with... whole new gen... ...A waiting to be tapped, it was boun... ...meone, somewhere, that ...scitating the ape franchise might just ...

When Tim Burt... — whose fanboy enthusiasm for campy... ...a Fifties and Sixties was w... ...known — was first approached about a... ...w Of The Apes, the directo... ...from Sleepy Hollow, was 'plenty wary'. ... ...now, he couldn't resist... ...e pleasures to be had from tackling t... ...ht glo-ries of the s...

Raised i... ...hadow... ...ney's Burbank Studios, and having c... ...h... youth-ful obse... ...n with misfits, h... ...or films and hammy actors, Burton... ...erfected his refreshingly off-centre worldview. He's the goth whizz who broug... ...such fan-tastical treats as *Edward Scissorhands*, *Mars Attacks!* and *Beetleju...* ...f anyone can make the cinema-going population all monkey-feely all over a... ...it's him.

But as the curators and watchers of web-related *Phantom Mena...* ...*Lord Of The Rings* activity have already experienced, sci-fi/fantasy enthusia... ...uchy lot. Get it wrong and Burton will be flamed for millennia. Get it ri... ...an entirely new *Planet...* while simultaneously satisfying the fana... ... have conquered a genre, appeased his muse, and resurrect... ... as a *Batman*-like, modern-day franchise.

'The thing is,' Burton says in a break after abusing As... ...Wahlberg, 'I love... the original. I was not interested in making a B-movie... ...sequel.' Burton turns

im burt... couldn't resist the perverse... pleasures to be ha... from tac...ing the big-budge... glories o... the sacred ape

away for a moment to d... ...with simian'd Lisa Marie on the draping of her w... waisted ape dress. 'T... calls, 'Helena's ready...'

Burton bounds a... ...ack, 'I guess it was the material. It must have ... something about ...ng apes. ...nk I found that was just very intriguing.'

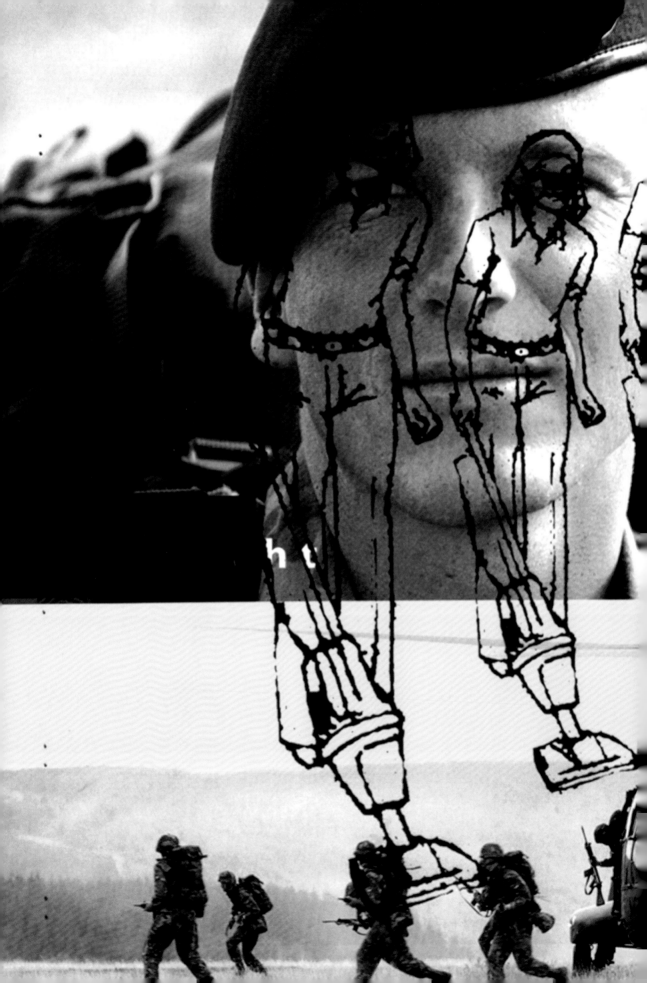

AGNÈS DECOURCHELLE

Agnès Decourchelle spent part of her childhood in Bangui, the capital of the Central African Republic. She says that this gave her a strong sense of smell, colour and light. She studied at the Ecole Nationale Supérieure des Arts Décoratifs in Paris, and she later studied communication art and design at the Royal College of Art, London. She now lives in Paris where she works as an illustrator. Her clients include Wallpaper, World of Interiors, Condé Naste Traveller, *Opéra National de Paris, Carolina Herrera,* Etapes *and the* New York Times.

"I began keeping sketchbooks on a daily basis in my first year of art school. Up until then most of my drawings were on sheets of paper and in notebooks at school. For me, the pleasure in keeping a sketchbook is the pleasure of drawing, research, exercise, practice and observation. A sketchbook is a tool for communicating and exchanging ideas, the inspiration for my work, a collection of moments.

The technique I use – pen, ink, watercolour – depends on the subject or the place in which I am drawing. It can simply be a matter of convenience, or my choice may depend on which medium will best convey an emotion, the light or the atmosphere.

I travel with my sketchbooks. I have one very small one that I keep with me wherever I go. I have bigger ones that I sit down to, taking more time to draw bigger scenes with more fastidious attention to detail. Some go quickly, others last for months. Sometimes I stick pictures in for reference and I try colour shading techniques as if working out a palette. I write down ideas, times, weather, phone numbers, quotations, references – anything that relates to the page I am drawing. One rule I have is never to cut out a page, even if a drawing doesn't look good.

Drawing in public places makes me feel uncomfortable for the first few minutes while I settle down. Then, when they see me drawing, people come up to me and it can be fun to have a chat. It's easier to make contact when drawing than when taking photographs. I only once had a problem, when sketching workers in a Moroccan souk – they didn't want to have their faces drawn by a woman."

ABOVE / *Self-portrait*

RIGHT / Research for *Vue sur la Ville* annual calendar, 2007

OVERLEAF / Travel sketchbook to Morocco, 2001

60

TOP ROW / Travel sketchbook from Barcelona, 2003; Type research for portfolio, 2007

MIDDLE ROW / Drawings from a trip to Korea and research for *Vue sur la Ville* annual calendar, 2006–07; Research and preparatory drawing for an illustration commission by *Condé Nast Traveller*, 2006

BOTTOM ROW / Birds and flowers market, Ile de la Cité, Paris, 2006; Research for greeting cards, 2007

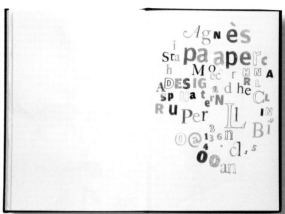

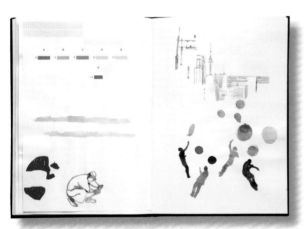

DOMINIC
DEL TORTO

Dominic del Torto is an artist, designer, animator and illustrator based in London. He works in a variety of media, including photography, photomontage, video, drawings and print, making entertaining work for TV and the web. His clients include BT, Virgin, Ford and Oasis.

"I was a very serious artist as a child, drawing super heroes, imaginary animals, souped-up cars, spaceships and aliens. My sketchbooks usually ended up as target practice for air rifles and home-made bows and arrows. I started keeping sketchbooks seriously while studying at Chelsea School of Art.

Then my sketchbook was with me wherever I went, which was usually the pub. I'd draw people and scenes. Over time I gradually began looking outwards less, and my drawing came more and more from my own imagination, like the drawings I made as a child. My observations now have more to do with the way people behave and how this makes me feel, rather than how things look.

My sketchbook is like an approving henchman – no matter how stupid or ill conceived an idea, sentiment or execution, my sketchbook always approves and allows me to continue the journey, wherever it leads. It is a constant ally in my never-ending war against emptiness and logic.

I don't like to be caught without a sketchbook and a camera. You never know when inspiration will strike – journeys and new environments are often very inspiring.

An artist I met recently said she thought my drawings were 'sad'. Generally people think my work is funny, but she's right, there is a sadness behind the class clown, who looks for approval by making a joke out of everything."

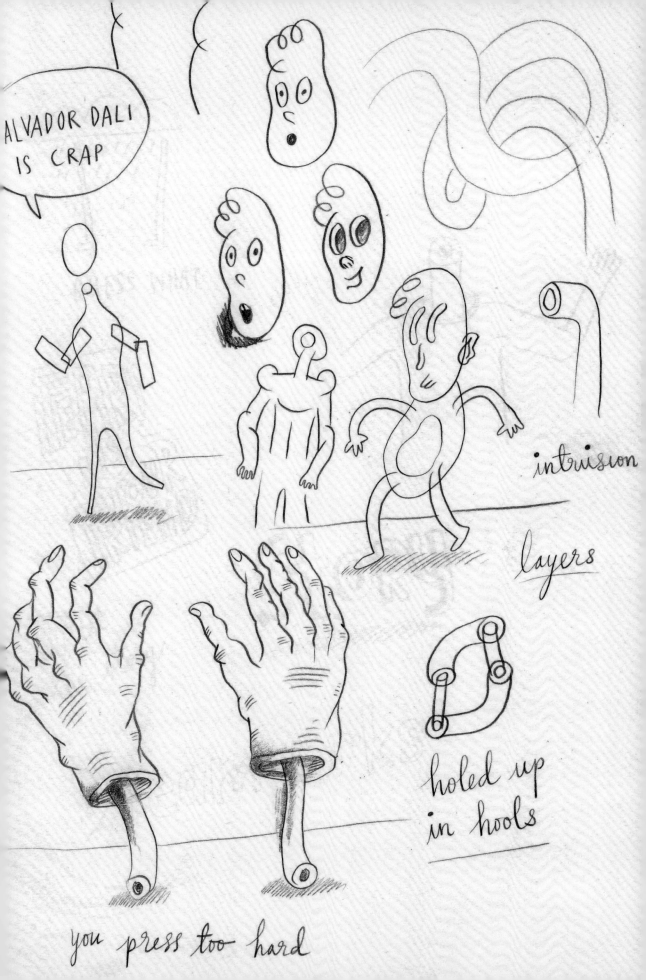

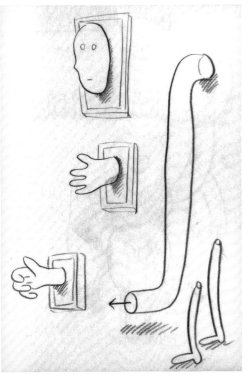

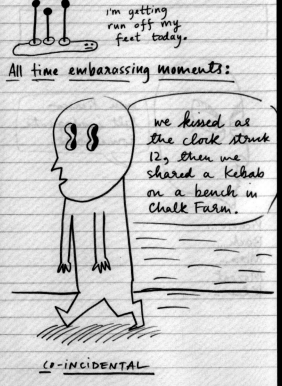

HENRIK DELEHAG

Born in Stockholm, Henrik Delehag moved to London in 2003 where he met Ben Carey, and together they set up Benrik Limited. Described as an "ideas factory for books, films and art", Benrik's mission is to spread a little welcome anarchy in people's lives. This creative duo specializes in guidebooks for modern living. This Diary Will Change Your Life, *now in its fourth edition, gives its disciples a life-changing task every day, ranging from "today do a runner" to "today propose to a complete stranger". The even more ambitious* Lose Weight! Get Laid! Find God! The All-in-One Life Planner *proposes a complete life plan from 0 to 100, including "losing your virginity" aged 17 and "uncovering the meaning of life" at 97.*

"I started keeping a sketchbook when I got tired of having my work on separate pieces of paper. I must have been about twelve. Actually, I would not even describe it as a sketchbook – it's really a book. I find sketches untidy. Ideas become better if you treat them well. Knowing that they will be treated well, they keep on coming.

I keep my sketchbooks for a long time. They get to be thick, like a bible. When the binding can no longer be repaired with gaffer tape I give the sketchbook a funeral in the family grave of my bottom drawer.

I tend not to glue too much stuff into sketchbooks. I want everything to be done by my hand or, on rare occasions, by someone else's hand. I don't like colour either. Colours are not black and white.

My sketchbook comes with me absolutely everywhere. It has become part of my identity and leaving it at home amputates part of me.

The most unusual entry in my sketchbook? A little ad I found on the tube. It says: 'BEARD CARESS for ladies [telephone number].'

I'm a sketchbook exhibitionist. I'm not at all precious about who gets to have a look. My most private writing, however, has become much smaller with the years. If I see someone squinting at that I give them a smack."

Can you see my school from up there?

HELL YEAH

NAKED MORE GUY

FACE OF AN

BENRIK

SELLING YOU!

MEANING WELL

LOVE OF GOD

WHAT ON EARTH AM I DOING ??????

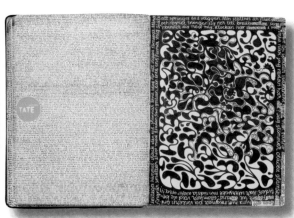

Marion Deuchars studied illustration and printmaking at Duncan of Jordanstone College of Art and Design, Dundee, Scotland, and the Royal College of Art, London. In 1989 she graduated with an MA (RCA) with distinction. She set up an art and design studio with some fellow RCA students and continues to work from a multi-disciplinary studio in north London. Since graduating, Deuchars has worked with major design and advertising agencies worldwide. Her commercial work has covered a varied range of illustration, including corporate literature, publishing, editorial, packaging, retail, advertising, design for web, brand development, craft and architecture. She has been a member of Alliance Graphique Internationale (AGI) since 2001.

"I started keeping a sketchbook when I was eight years old. The only paper I bought was sketchbooks from our (one and only) local art shop, owned by a strange, quietly spoken man with ginger hair. My sketches included lots of drawings of saccharine furry animals and portraits of Tony Hart, Neil Diamond and Marlon Brando. I must have been a weird kid.

When I started keeping them, my sketchbooks were very personal. They may have been a way for me to track my development. Now they are far more practical. I use them to solve problems.

In my first year at art college I had a big, luxurious Daler hardback, which I treasured and chopped and changed, adding the usual bus tickets, coffee-stained notes and the like. It was like a favourite soft toy, and I treasured and loved it. The problem I had was how to translate my cherished sketches into artwork. This was always a dismal failure – the minute the idea was removed from my beloved sketchbook, it died.

Now I tend to fill my sketchbooks fairly quickly with ideas and lists more than pictures. The thing that I love about them now is that I can write or scribble down ideas and I don't have to resolve them all. Some can stay on the back burner for years, slowly coming to life.

I like to buy sketchbooks on location. When I travelled to the States a while back, I drew on a postcard every day for a month and posted them all to a friend.

For me producing a sketchbook is a bit of trickery. I trick myself into thinking it's just a little sketchbook. That no one will see it. I can draw in it, write what I like in it. This, surreptitiously, allows me to create pictures without inhibition. However, the reality is that underneath that veil, I hope to produce something truly worthwhile."

RIGHT / Page from Cuba Sketchbook Diary, 1999.
"Eliana was my Spanish 'Professora Particular'.
She used to draw on the streets on my way to and
from her class in Vedado, Havana"

Eliana

SATURDAY	10-00	3 HOURS
MONDAY	2-00pm	3 HOURS
TUES. 17th	1-00	3 HRS
WED 18	11-00	3 HRS
THURS 19th	4-00pm	3 HRS
FRID. 20th	11-00	3 HRS

THIS PAGE, CLOCKWISE FROM TOP LEFT / Page from Cuba Sketchbook Diary, 1999. "My shopping list for the day and a dog that used to hang around outside my door"; Page from Cuba Sketchbook Diary, 1999. Two men talking on El Malecón, Havana; Page from Cuba Sketchbook Diary, 1999. Taxi, Havana; Working sketches for the *Guardian*, 2006: "Authority and the Abuse of Power"

RIGHT / Working sketch for the *Guardian*, 2006: "Extremism. Can Sexual Inadequacy Turn Angry Young Men into Killers?"

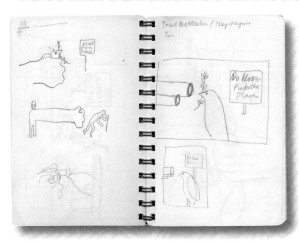

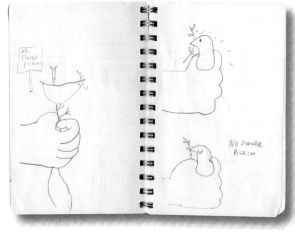

/Richard still life.
Killeen black + red/orange.

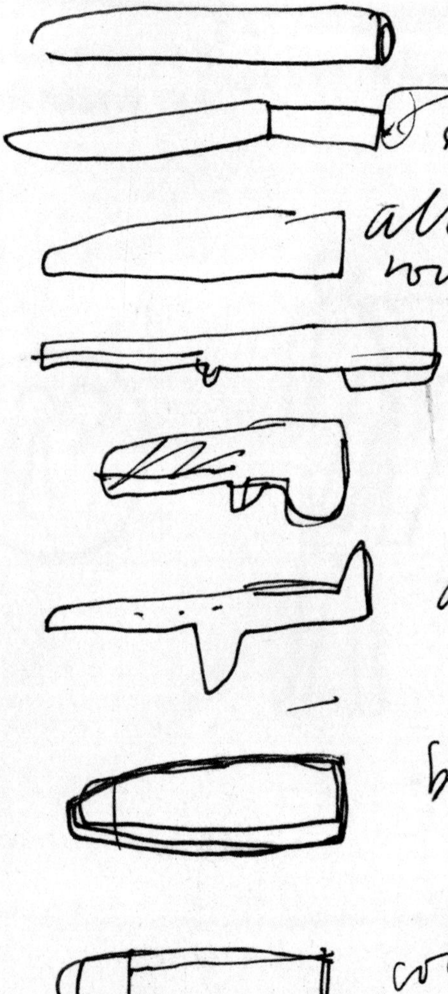

baloon

knife.

all male
rocket

Gun.

red chalk
on grey

aeroplane
rocket
gun
rifle.
penis.

aeroplane

bullets

cocks.

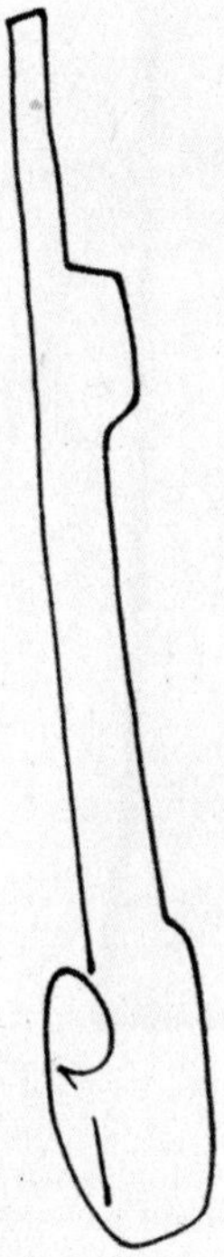

One big
rocket launcher.

BOM   BO

ANDREA
DEZSÖ

Illustrator Andrea Dezsö was born in Transylvania and now lives in New York City where she is assistant professor of media design at Parsons The New School for Design. Her artwork and writing have appeared in the New York Times, McSweeney's, Esopus, Blab *and* Print.

"In 1992, while still an undergraduate, I was an exchange student at Middlesex University, London, and it was there that I first came across sketchbooks. Confessional, reflective, journal-like sketchbooks were encouraged. I still have my first sketchbook. I realized that I felt more comfortable working on pages in books, pages that can be turned and hidden, or revealed as separate images and hung on a wall.

Even though I am aware that people might eventually look at my sketchbooks, it's not the same feeling of unilateral exposure as when one looks at a picture on a wall standing by itself. Coming across the same work in a book is more like a game of hide-and-seek.

It can be hard to find the perfect sketchbook, and I am very particular about the kind of paper used, the feel of it, the smoothness, the shade, the transparency. If it's a lined book, I look at the colour of the lines and the amount of space between them. Once I find a sketchbook I like, I stock-pile and replenish frequently for fear that I will never come across it again.

I always carry a small and thin brown (Muji-brand) lined notebook everywhere I go. These are my least composed sketchbooks, the ones I use on a daily basis whether I am in town or out of the country. They are all dated and numbered on the inner front cover and I decorate each cover differently, using drawing, painting, printing, stickers, found labels or paper cutouts.

I use a small Moleskine when travelling, as they fit in my back pocket. On long flights or when sitting on a beach I like to sketch what I see. The familiarity of sketching is a way of grounding myself, it allows me to retreat from the anxiety of an unknown environment, directing my attention with purpose and clarity towards a singular object of my choosing, and I can filter out everything else. When travelling I also carry a small camera and take photographs, but drawing is something I think about. It has a different personal involvement than the time investment of taking a photo.

For me sketchbooks have no filters, everything goes in."

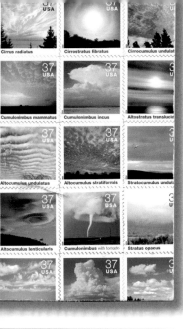

Cirrus radiatus | Cirrostratus fibratus | Cirrocumulus undulat

Cumulonimbus mammatus | Cumulonimbus incus | Altostratus translucid

Altocumulus undulatus | Altocumulus stratiformis | Stratocumulus undula

Altocumulus lenticularis | Cumulonimbus with tornado | Stratus opacus

Visitor

ROGER & GALLET
PARIS

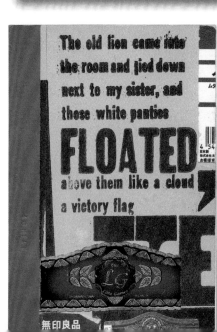

The old lion came into
the room and lied down
next to my sister, and
these white panties
FLOATED
above them like a cloud
a victory flag

無印良品

BELOW / Lined Muji notebook including shopping lists, to-do lists with completed chores crossed out, reminders, thoughts, anxieties, 2004

BOTTOM / Small Moleskine sketchbook. Sketches of mountain goats in Montana. Pen on paper, 2005

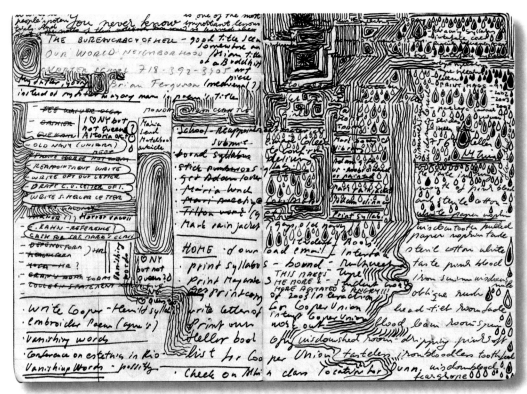

BELOW / Small Moleskine sketchbook. Sketch of a field on the Ucross Ranch in Wyoming. Pen on paper, 2005

BOTTOM / Small Moleskine lined notebook spread. Migraine-calendar between 22 November and 15 January, 2005

79

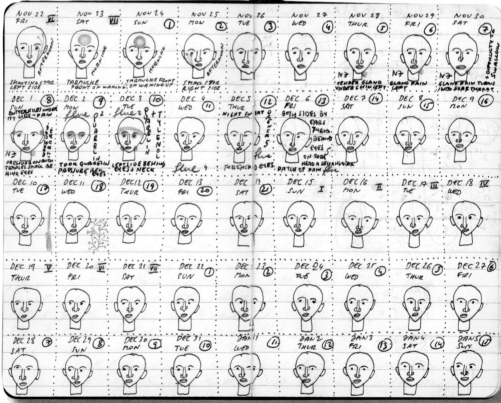

BELOW / Small Moleskine sketchbook. "Drawing with left hand while riding on the New Jersey Turnpike." Pen on paper, 2004

BOTTOM & OPPOSITE TOP LEFT / California Book. Small Moleskine sketchbook. "Observation sketches of chickens at our friends Tim and Kelly's farm in California." Pen on paper, 2004

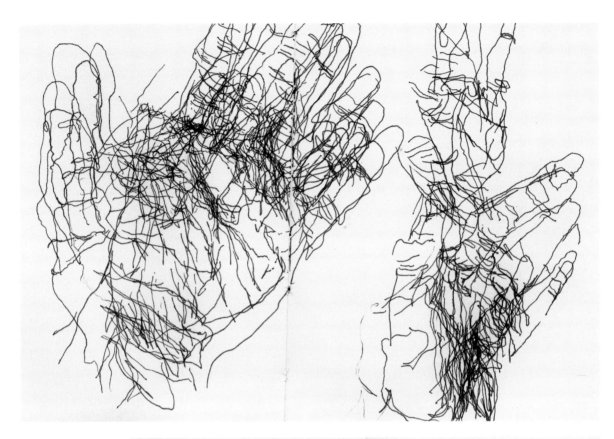

BELOW RIGHT / California Book. Small Moleskine sketchbook. "Observation sketch of a strawberry plant at Tim and Kelly's farm in California." Pen on paper, 2004

BOTTOM / Small Moleskine sketchbook spread. Drawing of the lines of the left palm; Study of a dead accordion-winged locust, Ucross ranch in Wyoming. Disposable black micropigment pen on paper, 2004

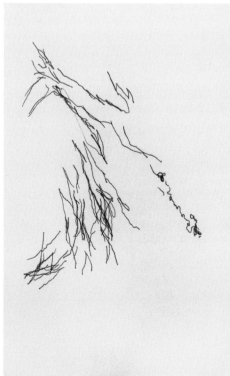

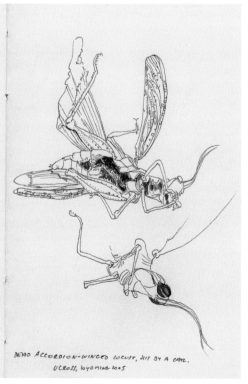

PAULUS M. DREIBHOLZ

Typographer and graphic designer Paulus M. Dreibholz was born in 1977 in Graz, Austria, and moved to London to study communication design. Having been awarded a BA in graphic and media design from the London College of Printing (London College of Communication) and an MA in communication design from Central Saint Martins College of Art & Design, London, he set up his own practice. He is currently an associate lecturer at Central Saint Martins and at the University of Applied Arts in Vienna.

"I began using sketchbooks when studying graphic design. We were encouraged to keep a visual diary, a record, a journal of some sort. It was not so much a tool, more a playground, a collection of bits and bobs produced while working on a project.

It became a means of relaxation, almost meditation, although I wouldn't have labelled it as such back then. My friend would call and ask whether I wanted to come around to her place to work on some sketchbook pages. It sounds sort of weird now, but we did it as others would play a board game or take a stroll through the park. It was about composition, colours, layouts and simple visual energy. Her pages were always full of a happy energy, lively and colourful, whereas mine ended up much less colourful but more pragmatic.

There were no goals. We'd draw, paint and tape around things. We didn't have an agenda or format, and our books were different shapes and sizes and made of different paper, etc. We hadn't yet figured out how to use the sketchbook effectively and more systematically. It was a collection of thoughts, experiments, notes from lectures, graphic ephemera we found and other things.

I can literally, and visually, trace my life back in my sketchbooks. I use them extensively and much more pragmatically these days, but they are still collections of private and professional ideas, thoughts and memories, a tool to define and refine things.

When an idea comes to me I note it down. I rarely have to revisit a sketchbook for ideas – by drawing or writing them down I will have positioned them more prominently in my head.

Even if I have progressed with a design to the digital stage I'll come back and draw the basic concepts on paper again.

The sketchbooks also help me to organize my life and ideas. I make extensive lists of things to do in terms of projects, and I then tick them off (or cross them out) as I complete them.

My sketchbook is a tool and, as such, is precious, but it's not something pretending to be something else. These days I rarely stick anything into my sketchbook unless it is connected with a strong memory and doesn't interfere with the use of it."

RIGHT / Cover of sketchbook used between
10 September 2007 and 1 March 2008

IN CASE YOU FIND THIS BOOK
PLEASE RETURN IT TO

PAULUS M. DREIBHOLZ

111 SHACKLEWELL LANE
LONDON E8 2EB
UK

ALTERNATIVELY CALL ME ON
+44 (0)7932 008 917   (UK)
+43 (0)676 591 7921   (AT)

OR SEND AN EMAIL TO
PAULUS@DREIBHOLZ.COM

THANK YOU!

BELOW / Unused first calligraphic scribbles for *Tasting Notes* magazine

BOTTOM / Typographic experiments

RIGHT / Various: To-do lists, crossed out once dealt with and solved; sketch of a typeface; early stages of typeface designs at different sizes; day-to-day notes and references

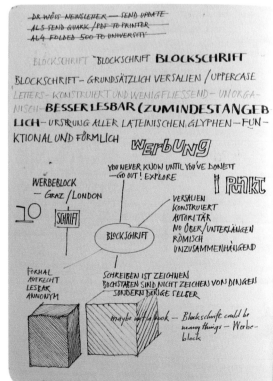

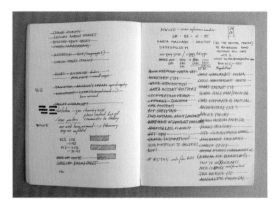

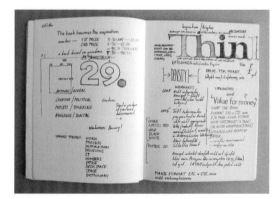

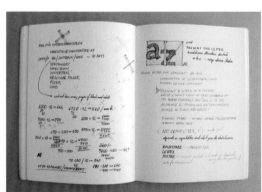

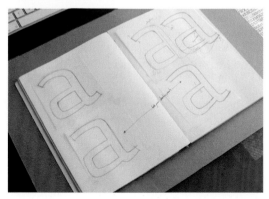

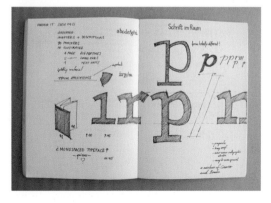

Henrik Drescher was born in Copenhagen, Denmark. At the age of 12 his family emigrated to the US where he later attended the School of the Museum of Fine Arts, Boston. After one term and on the advice of his tutors he left and began working as a freelance illustrator. Later he travelled extensively throughout the US, Europe and Central America, keeping notebooks and sketchbooks, which are the foundation for his illustration portfolios. He currently lives between western China and Canada. His son, Joakim Drescher, was born in Denmark in 1986 and has lived in many different places – the US, Indonesia, New Zealand and China – and is currently living in Denmark. In between reading books and drawing feverishly he is looking into different schools.

Henrik Drescher "I began keeping a sketchbook in high school at the age of 15. They are my ideas' filing cabinets. I use them to collect images, which I spill into commercial commissions and personal pictures.

I've kept sketchbooks for many years. I'll put them down and pick them up later. But in general I work from beginning to end and then start a new one. Some are theme-based, some are just day-to-day idea logs. In recent times I've worked on folded pieces of paper, which I bind together every month. I curate the contents – generally what I put in there is 'important' to my commercial and private pictures work. Sometimes, although rarely, I just record scenes and people.

I'm always looking to finalize my sketchbooks in a published form. I've been fortunate enough to do this in a few cases. One example is called *Turbulence*, others are limited editions based on my notebook pages. I always have a sketchbook with me. If I don't, then I make one. I try to refrain from personal writing because I usually regret it whenever I do confessional journalling. The sketchbooks are what I do, they're extended stories and image poems."

Joakim Drescher "I began keeping sketchbooks not that long ago, actually, maybe around the age of 16. At first I didn't do it very seriously, just collecting materials, ideas and storylines. Then, about two years ago, they became more important. My sketchbooks are a visual diary, a place to put impressions, thoughts that pass through the mind. Key words takes shape here and later turn into new things, whole stories or projects. For instance, a phrase such as 'and if I have fear' turns into a storyline about those you love. A whole storyline or project can come from one word or sentence – without a sketchbook they would pass by and be buried. I draw pretty much all the time. I guess some would say I'm a graphomaniac."

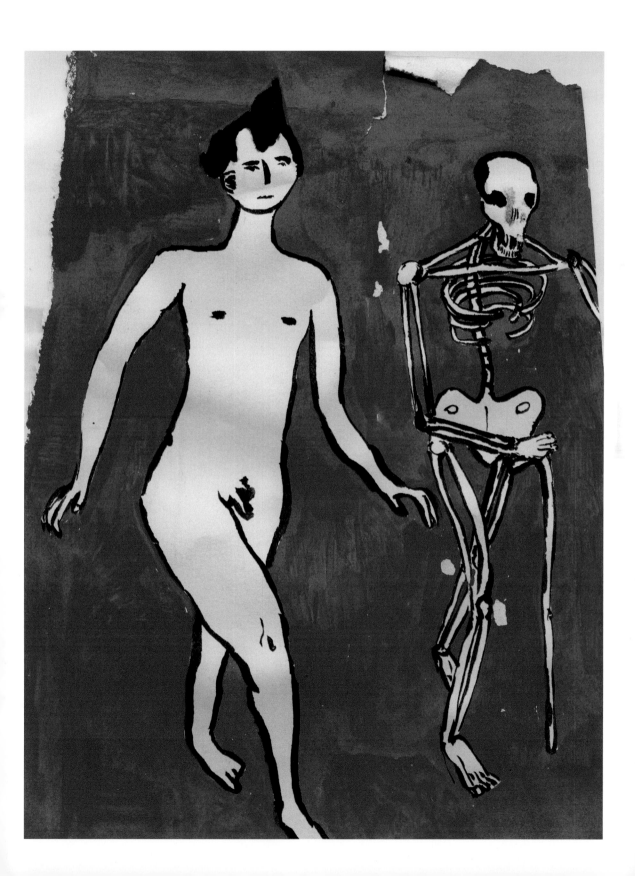

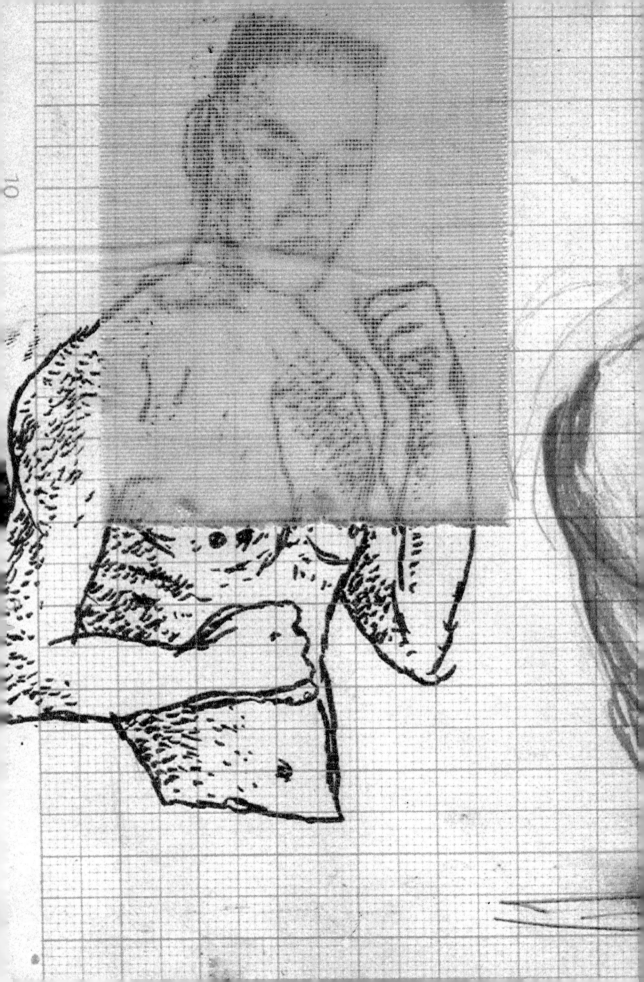

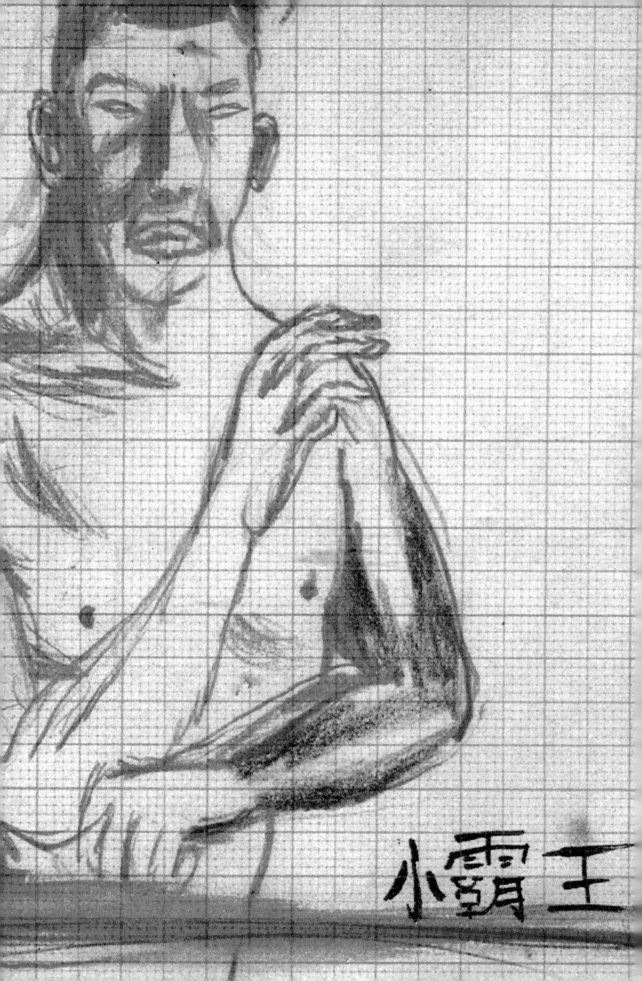

小霸王

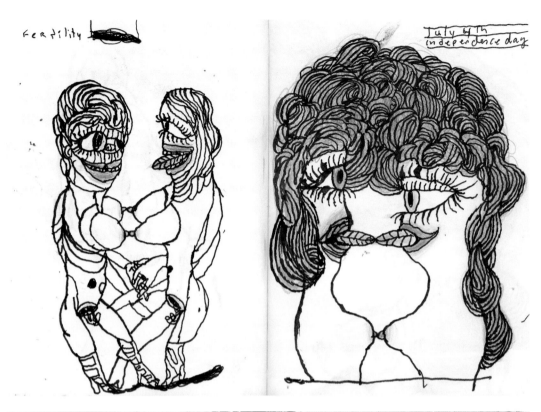

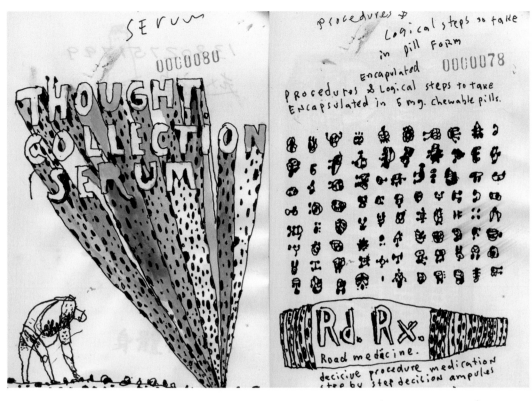

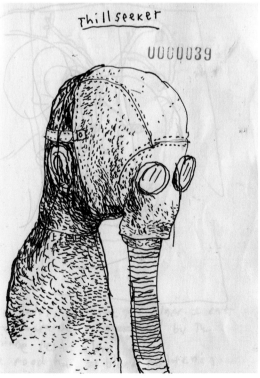

ED
FELLA

Ed Fella, a former commercial artist (1957–87) currently teaches graphic design at the California Institute of the Arts in Los Angeles. A book of his photographs and lettering, Letters on America, *was published by Princeton Architectural Press in 2000. He was a finalist for the National Design Awards in 2001, and in 2007 was an AIGA Design Legends gold medallist. His work is in the National Design Museum and the Museum of Modern Art, New York.*

"In 1976 an artist friend gave me a sketchbook, saying, 'Even though you're a designer, you think like an artist and should keep a sketchbook.'

The first sketchbooks started out as a sort of daily journal, but with collaged bits of type, product wrappers and fragments of hand-coloured photocopies. After the first one I never stopped making and keeping them, although the focus and intent of each new sketchbook changed – the diary-type journals lasted just a few years and the books became completely impersonal with studies of form and text, in most cases without any subject or meaning.

For me these books are a means of detachment. They are a discharge, a continuation of form studies based on my 30 years of work as a professional illustrator and graphic designer (lettering and typography). They are mostly non-objective or 'deconstructed' form drawings, decorative and embellished with techniques I learned in my commercial art illustration practice. They reference a history (late nineteenth to mid-twentieth century) that was before my time, but one that I find rich in possibilities for reworking.

I have never been without an ongoing sketchbook or two during the last 32 years. In that time I have accumulated over a hundred books. My sketchbooks fall into three broad categories: pure collage; lettering (in four-colour ballpoint with prismacolour pencil); mixed media form studies and fragments of illustration with some lettering and collage.

I have larger-format collage books that stay in the studio but I am never without a portable sized book that goes everywhere with me. Since the sketchbooks are with me all day they are always 'travelling', and are added to in all those odd moments during the course of a day. If there is enough light I draw during lectures and concerts, and in social settings such as waiting for or after a meal, while watching TV or listening to the news on the radio, or when I'm just sitting on a park bench, relaxing."

ABOVE / Ed Fella in his studio at CalArts in Los Angeles, 2007

RIGHT / Prismacolour pencil drawing from a 1984 sketchbook

BELOW / Four-colour ballpoint pen with white and yellow prismacolour pencil on paper from a 2004 sketchbook

RIGHT & OVERLEAF / Collages from a 1983 sketchbook

Delaware Water Gap

Photo by A. Dillahunty

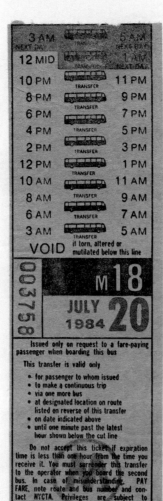

3 AM NEXT DAY   5 AM NEXT DAY
12 MID   1 AM NEXT DAY
10 PM   11 PM
TRANSFER
8 PM   9 PM
TRANSFER
6 PM   7 PM
4 PM   5 PM
TRANSFER
2 PM   3 PM
12 PM   1 PM
TRANSFER
10 AM   11 AM
8 AM   9 AM
TRANSFER
6 AM   7 AM
TRANSFER
3 AM   5 AM
TRANSFER
VOID if torn, altered or mutilated below this line

003758

M18

JULY 20 1984

Issued only on request to a fare-paying passenger when boarding this bus

This transfer is valid only

- for passenger to whom issued
- to make a continuous trip
- via one more bus
- at designated location on route listed on reverse of this transfer
- on date indicated above
- until one minute past the latest hour shown below the cut line

Do not accept this ticket if expiration time is less than one hour from the time you receive it. You must surrender this transfer to the operator when you board the second bus. In case of misunderstanding, PAY FARE, note route and bus number and contact NYCTA. Privileges are subject to change.

UNAUTHORIZED USE, PURCHASE, OR SALE IS A CRIMINAL OFFENSE

New York City Transit Authority
S U R F A C E

Metro-North Commuter Railroad

OFF PEAK COACH

FAIRFIELD TO

NEW YORK

NO. MACH. 50

1 2 3 4 M

179526

SOLD SUBJECT TO TARIFF REGULATIONS F

NO. 51759

TKT. JUL 15 -84

New York City collage II

BELOW / Three collage pages from a 2002 sketchbook (Moleskine Accordion Fold). All fragments of posters from streets in Melbourne, Australia

BOTTOM LEFT / Four-colour ballpoint pen with yellow and blue prismacolour pencil, 2001

BOTTOM RIGHT / Four-colour ballpoint pen. Sketchbook from 1992

BELOW / Four-colour ballpoint
pen with yellow prismacolour
pencil. Venice, Italy, October 2002

101

ISIDRO FERRER

Isidro Ferrer was born in Madrid in 1963, and he set up his own studio in Huesca, Spain, in 1996. His work includes illustration, poster and editorial design and TV animation. He has taught illustration at the European Design Institute in Madrid and at the Eina School in Barcelona. He has published many books in France, Spain and Portugal and is a member of the Alliance Graphique International. His clients include El País, *Huesca Film Festival, Editorial Santillana, Canal+ and Volkswagen.*

"The oldest sketchbook I have is from 1983, when I was 20 years old, a student. I still have some folders with drawings and scattered notes made before this.

My memory is capricious and selective and for this reason I am determined to fence it in. I do my best to record my path, the signs and marks that show my progress and the point of my arrival. My drawings and writings are small milestones along the path, providing evidence of what I am living.

I try to hold moments so that I can bring them to life again, and I do it by means of my most accessible tool: drawing. I draw as I breathe, without consciousness, with conscience. I like to draw, compile and store. In the sketchbooks, which in some cases are like diaries, I order information that I have collected and which could be useful.

For me, it is very therapeutic to draw. I love the texture of the paper, the stroke of the pencil, the stroke on the paper, the tactile part of the action of drawing.

In the sketchbooks, I try to order my world, to upgrade information, to make a note of events, to write a list of works or a shopping list, to note down phone numbers, movies that I've seen, books I will read, quotes found in books I've read, discs that have seduced me...

My travelling and personal sketchbooks mark out this path, and sometimes they guide and support me.

Some of the sketchbooks are empty and others are full of drawings, of accomplices' words or notes about anonymous people. One part of my library is destined to keep these sketchbooks, both full and empty. The full ones are empty of space, and the empty ones are full of possibilities, because anything can lodge in their naked wombs.

I arrange my sketchbooks according to use. There are sketchbooks for recording thoughts and actions connected with my job – ideas, sketches and projects; and there are sketchbooks that have a more private use – these become companions on my journey, a place where I keep my impressions, reflections and quotes. There is often a cross-contamination between the two types of sketchbook, and it can be very difficult to establish the difference between them.

I usually fill the pages of my sketchbook in cafés or hotel rooms, starting with the passages that I have been gathering throughout the day.

I never have just one sketchbook – there are always two or three, which I usually add to privately, and they're always with me."

RIGHT / *It Is Forbidden to Introduce Infectious-Contagious Diseases.* Huesca, Spain, 5 February 2007

OVERLEAF / *The Bag or the Life.* São Paulo, Brazil, 19 March 2007

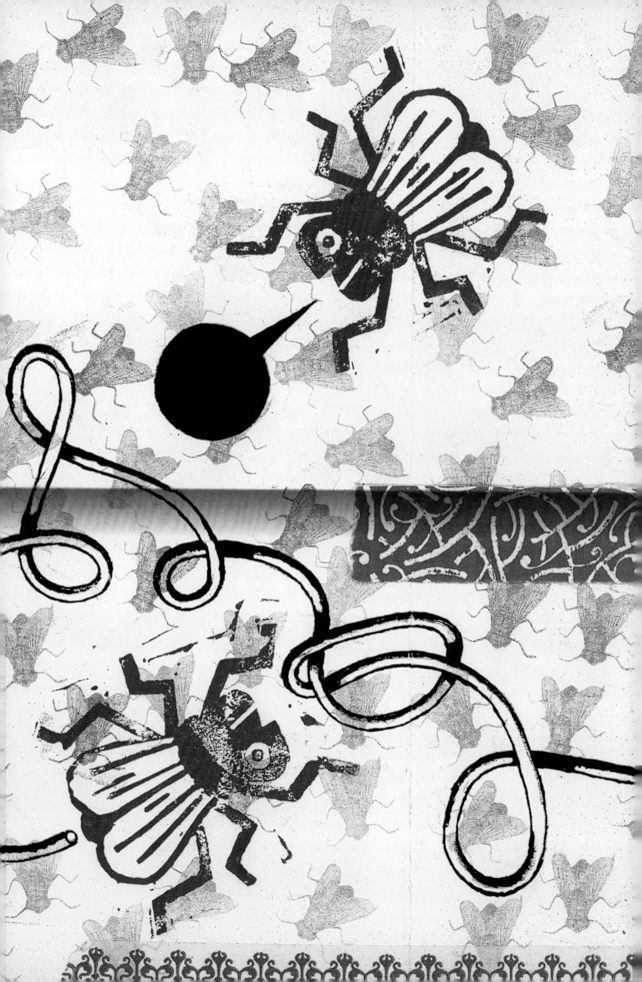

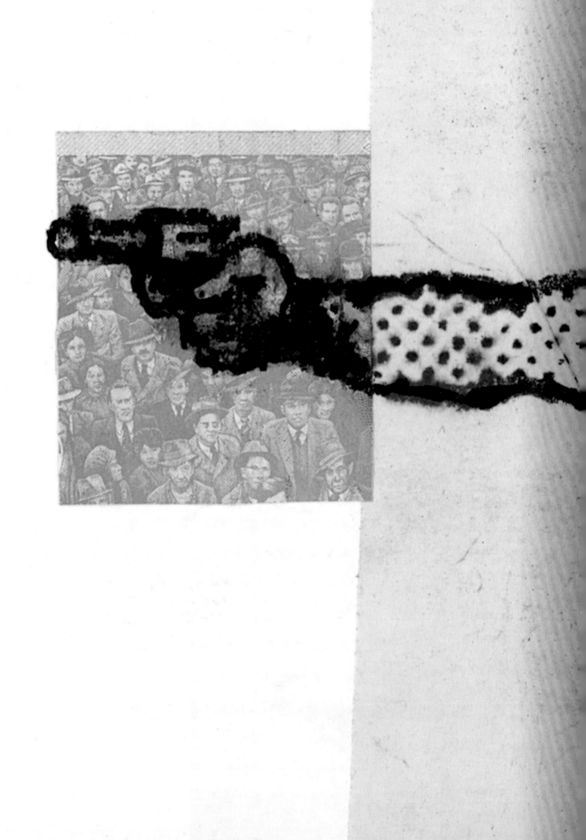

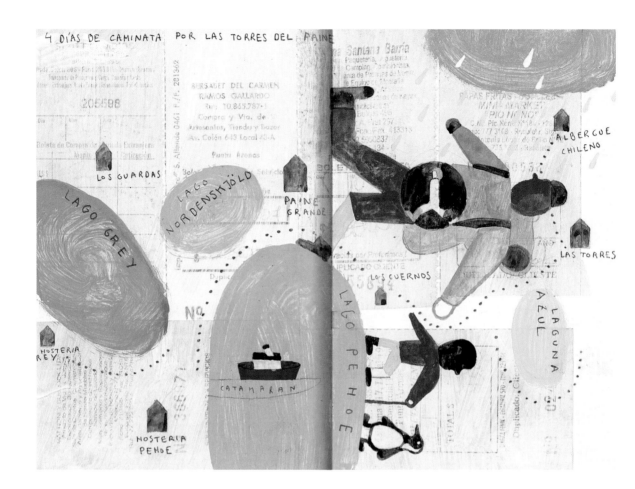

TOP ROW / *My bedroom.* Pau, France, 30 January 2007; *Violeta in the Roof.* León, Spain, 14 May 2007

MIDDLE ROW / *Is.* Huesca, Spain, 20 January 2008; *Null and Void.* Huesca, Spain, 3 January 2007

BOTTOM ROW / *Drawing a Line Seems to Be Easy.* Barcelona, Spain, 13 June 2007. *Fragile.* Zaragoza, Spain, 16 February 2006

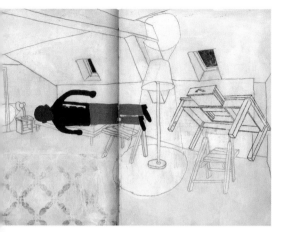

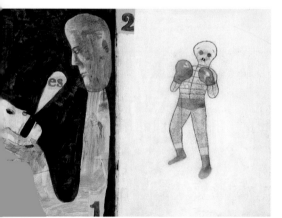

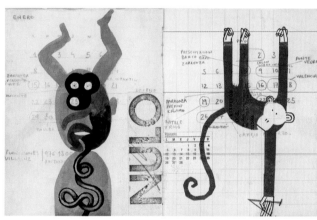

I AM LISTENING TO 'SKETCH FOR WINTER'
BY THE DURUTTI COLUMN.

Peter James Field is an artist and illustrator who lives and works in southern England. He studied art history at the University of East Anglia in Norwich, then lived in Japan for three years, working as a teacher. On his return he completed a degree in illustration at the University of Brighton and was the recipient of the John Lord sketchbook prize. Working freelance since 2005, his clients include Dazed & Confused, Time Out, *the* Independent, *the* Financial Times, Elle Decoration *and* Wallpaper.

"I've been keeping sketchbooks on and off as far back as I can remember. I've still got the early ones, dating from when I was about five. The interesting thing is they haven't changed much – then, as now, I was trying to look around and make something lasting from the mundane things that surrounded me. I wasn't trying to escape through narratives or fantasies, I was using drawing to digest and give meaning to the outside world.

Sometimes I feel that in keeping sketchbooks I'm documenting the world as I see it, like a kind of archivist, often using my sketches to search for connections in the small things that would otherwise be overlooked and forgotten. My sketchbook entries have captions, comments or opinions, which I often edit or simplify to put across the details I want to highlight.

My one rule for these sketchbooks is that there isn't a world paper shortage – so if in doubt, I just draw it. I can edit later. I have been known to make about 60 observations in one day. It serves a human need in me to draw, and it helps to keep me sane – but it's also important for other people to see it. It's by no means a completely private journal; I like to use it to communicate with others.

Thematically there is quite a cynical outlook and many of the captions are self-deprecating – but I think there is also warmth, sensitivity and a sense of humour. I guess I'm quite shy, and I can talk through my sketchbooks."

ABOVE / *Self-portrait,* September 2007

RIGHT / *Glasgow Central Station,* November 2007

OVERLEAF / *Tourists,* June 2007

They'll be ready. So will Gl

DEPARTURES BOARD, GLASGOW CENTRAL STATION.

TOURISTS, POOL

UAY.

BOURNEMOUTH BEACH. WINTER SEEMS DEFEATED.

EMPTINESS. FIRGROVE COURT FLATS, POOLE.

FUEL design group was founded in 1991 at the Royal College of Art. From the outset Damon Murray and Stephen Sorrell combined varied commissions with projects of their own – often containing thought-provoking messages, these bold graphic statements served as a developing manifesto. Since 1992 they have worked from their small studio in Spitalfields, London. In 2005 FUEL Publishing was formed within the group. FUEL's experience in book design and their close collaboration with authors on content have resulted in a range of eclectic and distinctive books, including the best-selling Russian Criminal Tattoo Encyclopaedia *series. They continue to work on both commercial and personal projects.*

"We don't keep sketchbooks as such, but have always sketched out ideas on scraps of paper in the studio. Keeping a sketchbook has always felt a bit like an art school chore.

Some people may find it to be second nature and effortless, but very often with sketchbooks we feel they can become too precious and considered. We tend to make drawings, doodles and notes on random pieces of paper or newspapers.

The drawings made on these newspaper cuttings are part of a lunchtime activity we occasionally fall into. It's our form of desktop graffiti. We keep the good ones but most of them end up in the bin. The main aim is to make us laugh."

ABOVE / Working drawing for painting, 2004

ALL IMAGES / *Untitled,* from newspapers

Second Test

England's Surrey all-rounder Rikki Clarke plays forward on his way to a maiden Test half-century during the afternoon session in Chittagong yesterday Photograph: Gareth Fuller/PA

available against England on Monday, speaks with the coach Otto Baric, right, in training in Leiria Jean-Paul Pelissier/Reuters

sights on England

s retur

Steve Davis, back among the game's

to snooker's top tal

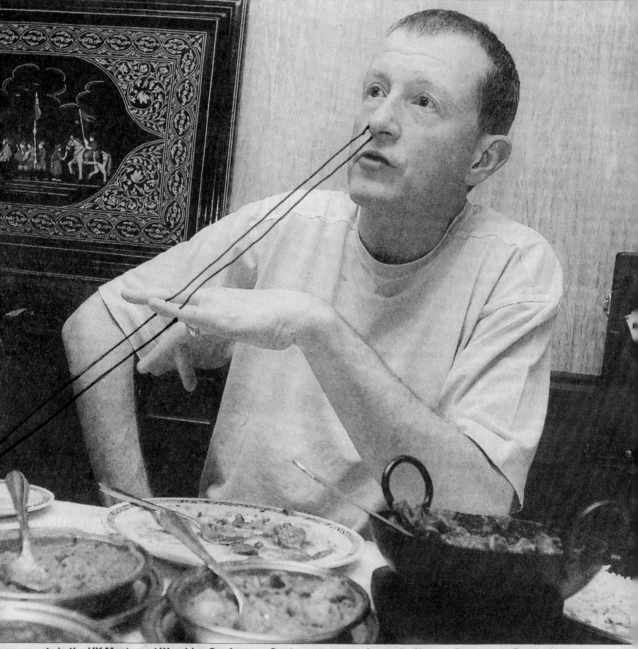

prospects in the UK Masters at Wembley Conference Centre over a curry in nearby Harrow Photograph: Tom Jenkins

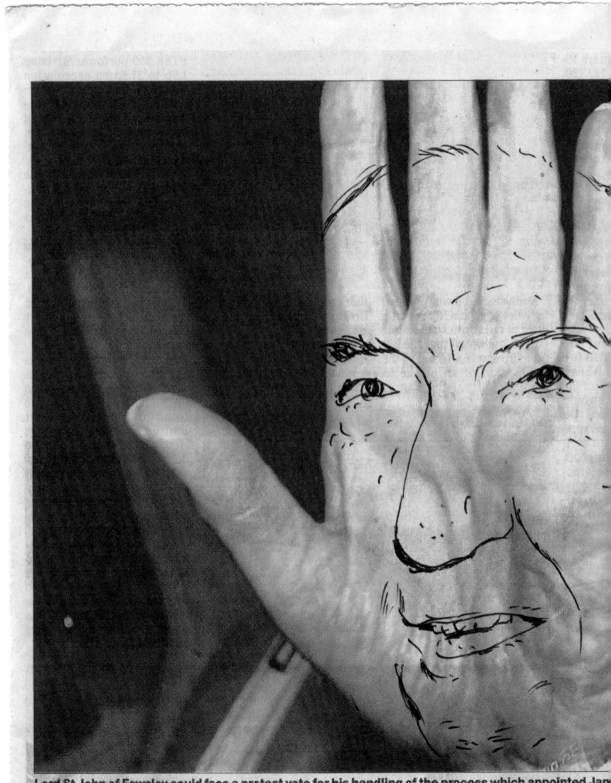

Lord St John of Fawsley could face a protest vote for his handling of the process which appointed Jan

elow left, son of Rupert Main photograph: Martin Argles

ANNA GIERTZ

Anna Giertz grew up on the Swedish Baltic Sea island of Gotland. She studied illustration and graphic design, completing an MA at Konstfack University College of Arts, Crafts and Design in Stockholm. She's a member of the Bravehat art collective and currently works as a freelance illustrator for various magazines, books and advertising. She is based in Stockholm, Sweden.

"I remember drawing cars on a bundle of loose papers when I was eight, lots and lots of different kinds of cars. I tried to sell them to neighbours, but I don't remember anybody buying any.

Sketchbooks are kind of private to me. I mostly draw on different paper, wasting huge amounts, and then I collect my sketches and put them into folders. I also use my sketchbooks when looking for ideas for commissions – the sketches can be a starting point.

I like grouping images that belong together. I compile different sketches in different folders, one for the 'almost ready' sketches, another for the 'almost the beginning of something' sketches, others for crazy things – colours, black and white, patterns, figurative drawings, etc.

I used to work only in black and white but now I work as much in colour as I do in black and white. Sketching in black and white is quicker, but it's more fun to work in colour. The colours used will often dominate a drawing and then it's easier to sketch in colour from the beginning. I like to use traditional materials – paper, pencils, charcoal, ink and brushes.

I can finish my more graphic sketches in less than half an hour, but some sketches are an ongoing project that I keep coming back to when I have some spare time.

I often buy sketchbooks when I'm travelling, which turn into notebooks as soon as I come home. I tear out the pages I want to save and transfer into folders. I don't usually show people my sketchbooks, as I think they would see my patterns and find me a bit repetitive, perhaps even stubborn, in what I draw."

ABOVE / Anna in the studio

RIGHT / Sketch to a text about "outsourcing" for the Swedish magazine *Odd at Large*, 2007

OVERLEAF / Part of a sketch for the poem *Do Not Go Gentle Into That Good Night* by Dylan Thomas, for the German magazine *Dong*, 2007; Personal work for Italian magazine *The End*, 2007

LEFT / *From a Tree.* Sketch for pattern. Personal work, 2007

BOTTOM / Personal work, 2006

BELOW LEFT / *See You.* Personal work, 2006. From a series of drawings with titles from old-school Depeche Mode songs

BELOW RIGHT / Personal work, 2007. Sketch for A1-size drawing for Cederteg Publishing

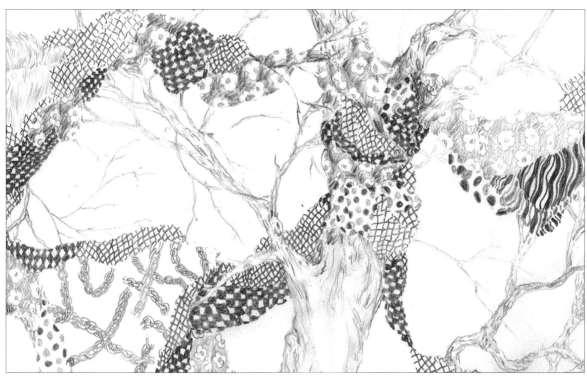

CHRIS GILVAN-CARTWRIGHT

Artist and illustrator Chris Gilvan-Cartwright studied at Central Saint Martins College of Art & Design and later completed an MA at the University of Brighton. He has exhibited his paintings in London and Edinburgh and his illustration clients include the BBC, the Sunday Times, *the* Telegraph, *the* Independent *and Penguin Books.*

"I once found an old accountancy ledger in a skip near Long Acre in London. There were entries going right back to the 1960s. It fascinated me to see the neat orderly rows of figures made during a decade of such social and creative movement. Above all I love the entry for 26 August 1966 – for the ledger it was just another set of mundane figures, but for me it was momentous, as it was the day I was born.

Twenty years ago I bought an 1839 edition of Lord Byron's work for ten pence in a second-hand bookshop on the Charing Cross Road. The pages were discoloured, and it even had a replica of a letter from Byron at the back. I've been using it as a sketchbook ever since. I love working on top of the text and images. The sketchbook has charted aspects of my work since I started using it.

Keeping a sketchbook on the go has meant different things at different stages in my life. When I was younger I used to hide behind it, and while out with mates at the pub I'd just be drawing away as people talked. Later it became a place where creative ideas could co-exist alongside shopping lists and reminder notes.

If I'm lecturing about my work I take my sketchbooks along for my students to leaf through so that they can see the unedited truth.

I need a medium that dries quickly so that the pages don't stick together. I love to work spontaneously and am very prolific, so watercolour and gouache are perfect media for my sketchbook.

I've always taken a sketchbook with me when travelling, choosing one that's light and quickly accessible. This enables me to work secretly behind the pillars in Delhi, and not be weighed down in the Nepalese Himalayas.

For me a sketchbook is a place for unedited creativity, somewhere that ideas can exist purely for their beauty. Nothing should be edited out."

RIGHT / Detail of *Frenzied and Gesturing.*
Gouache and Indian ink, 2007

...e...anfang ausm..., vermehrt... der von ihm ange-
nommene Platz... eine Reihe von Fragmenten — eine Schnur
orientalischer... zufällig zusammen gefügt — ...fern,
ließ ihn... ohne ihn an... Mehreres, als den... Gang
der Erzählung zu binden, völlige Freiheit...
was sein... Empfindungen oder... hervor-
brachte, und... er sich bei dieser Gelegen... durch...
sichten auf den Zusa... fesseln ließ, ...
mit welcher er... Absch... schönes... Jahrs-
... seiner eignen... begei... er sagt:
... Die Stelle, ... folg... Be... einzu... nd, noch
nicht bestimmt, werde... wenn ich...
... kein Abschrift zurückbehalten hab...

Als sein Biograph und Freund Moore w... dieses Früh-
lings in der Stadt wieder mit ihm... traf, fand er den
Enthusiasmus über ihn und seine... den er auf einer
so bedeutenden Höhe, sowohl in der... Welt... in
... Gesellschaft, verlassen hatte, wo möglich... allgemeiner
und... er geworden. In dem unmittelbar... liegenden
Kreise hatte allerdings vielleicht die Vertraulichkeit des Umgangs
sein gewöhnliche entzaubernde Wirkung he... racht. Es konnte
... fehlen, daß eine eigne Lebendigkeit... Rückhaltlosigke...
bei genauer Bek... ntschaft jenen Zaubern...
... ihn ... ige von entfernter... ... ...
... blickte, zer... ... mußte, während diese... schen Ideen,
... manche... ... Leserinnen... die... angen...
... amenlose... auf welche in... Gedichte... hingedeutet
... urde, ge... hatten, in... Eif... ... geriethe... dur... die
... nahe... orung u... de... ...muthlichen Gegenst... en jetziger
... eigu... ... Zärtlich... ... bestim... zu werden... ...e Geliebte
... ers sollte... ich fü... ndere eben... unbekannt

BELOW / *Two Head and Shoulders and a Fish.* Acrylic and printing ink, 1987

BOTTOM / *Untitled.* Acrylic, watercolour and ink, 1994

CLOCKWISE FROM TOP RIGHT /
Untitled. Gouache, 25 September
1989; *WSM Sunset.* Gouache and
acrylic, 1994; *WSM Dusk.* Gouache

and Indian ink, 1994; *Black Forest.*
Gouache, 27 September 1989;
Two Heads. Black gouache, 1989

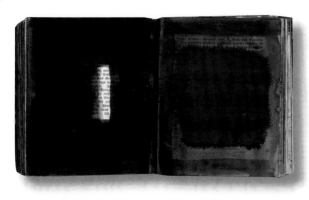

BRIAN GRIMWOOD

Brian Grimwood has been a successful illustrator for over four decades. In 1983 he founded the Central Illustration Agency (the CIA), which now represents some of the world's leading illustrators. His work is always instantly recognizable, and includes his famous Johnnie Walker man. His clients include Vogue, Manner Vogue, *the* BBC, *the* Times, *the* Listener, *the* Guardian, *and the* Telegraph.

"I have doodled in notebooks since I was a young boy growing up in Beckenham. Sometimes they are sketchbooks, sometimes diaries, sometimes both.

I made a conscious effort to keep a diary in 1975 and have managed more or less to keep it going every day since. I have shelves groaning with them – they are plainly bound, usually A4 in size and dated on the spine.

Generally they are neat, some with drawings done on serviettes from restaurant lunches tucked between the pages, and tickets from past exhibitions and various ephemera are also stuck in. I always write and draw with a pen, and anything personal is usually drawn rather than written. My sketchbook reflects my thoughts on any given day. I like the idea of documenting my life, or just recording something or somebody I'm interested in.

When at home I keep my sketchbook in the loo. This has been observed by the family who consider it fair game to look in. The stock joke is the entry 'my watch strap broke today' – it has been suggested that it would make a good title for my autobiography. I'm a poor sleeper and I can be found doodling in the early hours.

I have recently discovered Peter Beard and his sketchbooks – amazing! I can now see my sketchbooks introducing photographs and becoming messier.

I always have my sketchbook with me when travelling, working or on holiday. When I'm away there's less pressure, with no deadlines, and the drawings tend to look much better.

As part of a time line in my sketchbooks I record celebrities' deaths and make notes about news items. Because my sketchbooks double as a diary and are personal I don't usually show them to anyone outside of the family."

ABOVE / A recent picture taken in Little India in Singapore whilst working on a commission for Raffles Hotel, February 2008

RIGHT / A sketch for the cover of *Coffee with Charles Darwin,* one of a series of books published by Duncan Baird Publishers Ltd

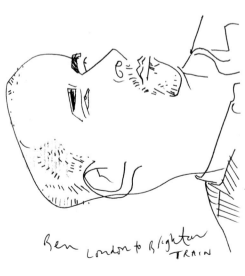

Ben London to Brighton
TRAIN

136

JOHNNY
HARDSTAFF

*Johnny Hardstaff is a moving image director with
Ridley Scott Associates, and a graphic designer/
illustrator with the Central Illustration Agency. He
studied at Central Saint Martins College of Art &
Design. He has designed and directed extended
promos for Radiohead's Amnesiac tracks "Pull/Pulk
Revolving Doors" and "Like Spinning Plates", and
commercials such as Orange (Paint) and subversive
long-format films for PlayStation's "History of
Gaming" and "Future of Gaming".*

"I have kept sketchbooks for 14 years, ever since graduating from Saint
Martins. Each one takes at least a year to complete. My sketchbooks are
incubators, a free and non-judgemental place to make mistakes and try
things out. I can regress into naive childishness within them. They seem
continually to get better and richer. They also seem to have got much
darker. The more recent ones are the most private.

I would like to think that the only thing that goes into my sketchbooks
are my original thoughts, and that it's the work of others that stays out,
and, largely, this is true, but of course there are always exceptions. As for
the ephemera that I sometimes paste in, it's my own particular logic system
that selects what gets laid down and what doesn't. It could be a price
sticker, a postmark, a printed scrap of colour, a name, a word….

I take a sketchbook literally everywhere. My current sketchbook has
been to Japan, Korea and parts of Europe. It's probably the first thing I
think to put in a bag when I travel anywhere at all.

I could never show anyone the current book, and those people close
to me now know never to look inside. Really, none of the sketchbooks
were ever for showing to anyone. They have simply recorded and charted
my life in the only manner that could be meaningful to me.

Once finished, once complete, my sketchbooks are worthless. In a
way they are themselves filters. They filter away the whimsical, the faddish
and the pointless. That way, the only useful sketchbook is the current one,
which carries forth with it interesting trains of thought."

ABOVE / *6MM Hate Head* © Johnny Hardstaff

ALL OTHER IMAGES / Johnny Hardstaff
sketchbook pages

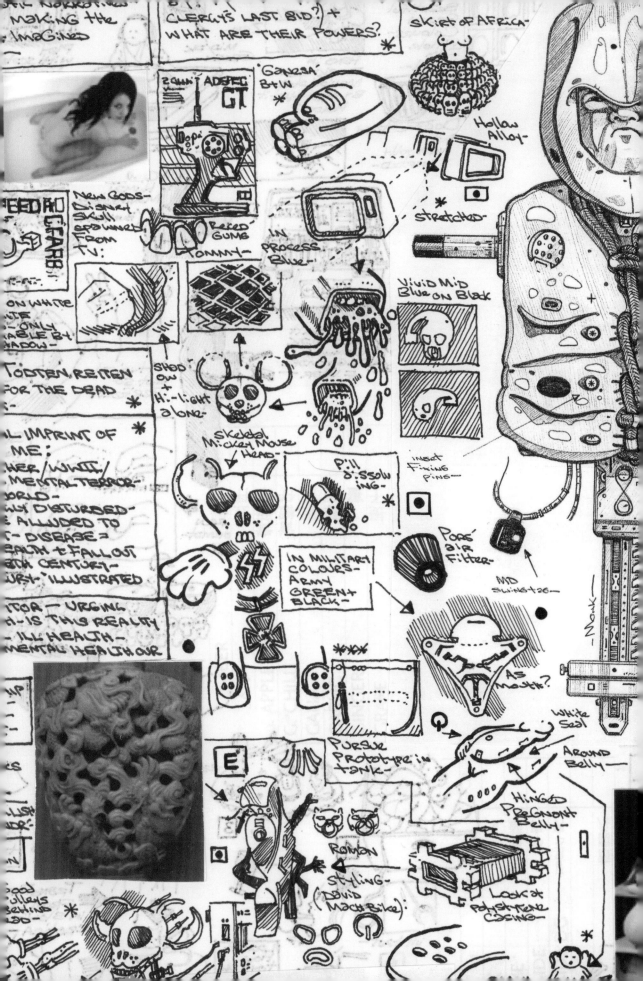

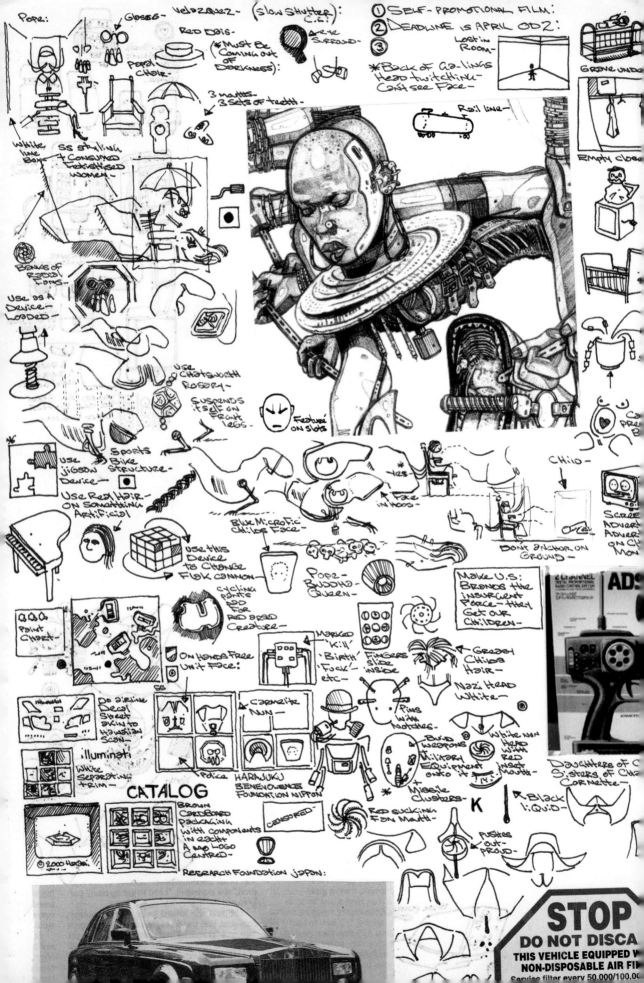

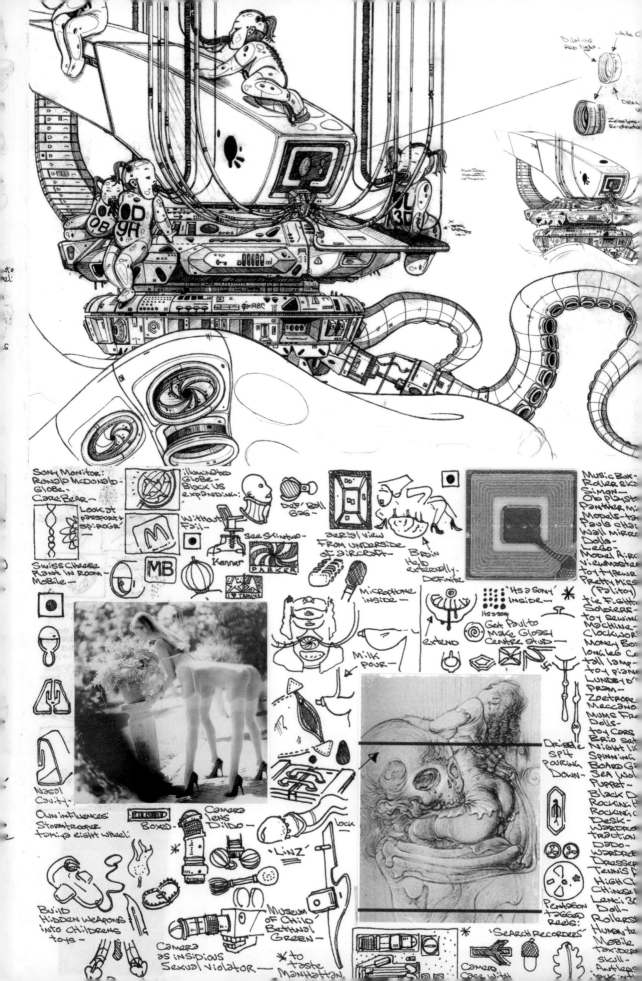

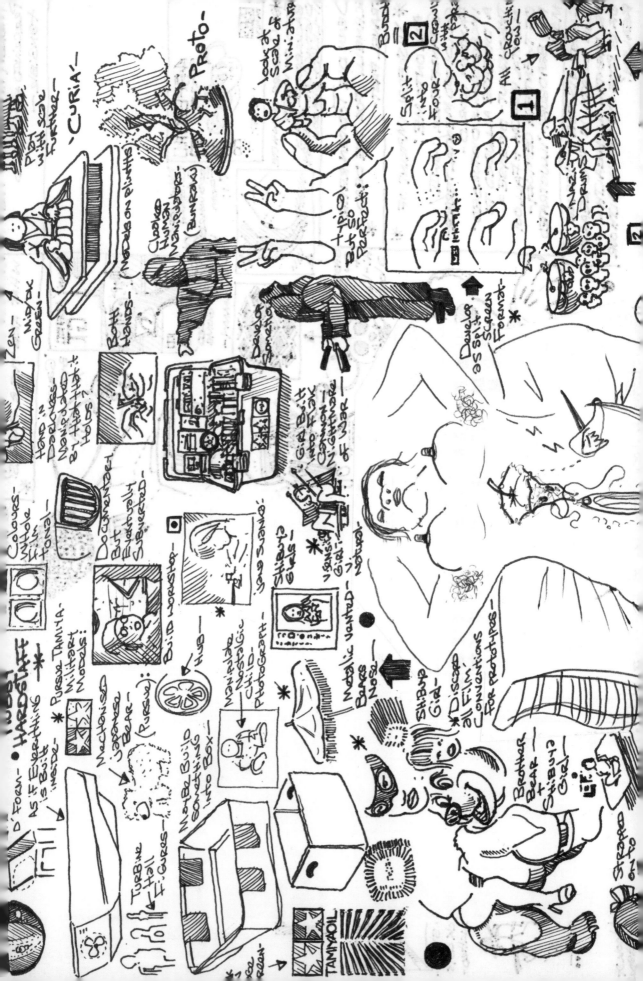

FLO
HEISS

Flo Heiss is creative director of Dare, an interactive marketing agency based in London. He was born in deepest Bavaria in 1969 and grew up in a place called Murnau, a place where people still wear lederhosen, a place so beautiful and conservative that at the age of 16 he felt the need to move to Northern Ireland. Thankfully, Warrenpoint in the 1980s, with its council estates and military checkpoints, proved to be the exact opposite of Murnau, and he thrived there. He later studied graphic design at the Royal College of Art, London.

"I have been drawing all my life, but it was in Ireland that I started drawing with a purpose.

I came back and finished school in Murnau. Then I moved to Augsburg to study graphic design, after an intense year of drawing at a private school located over a sex shop in Munich. During my four years at Augsburg I spent a year in the Italian town of Urbino, another place so beautiful and conservative that I felt the need to move back to somewhere a bit grittier. I graduated with a diploma in graphic design and finished my seemingly never-ending studies with an MA from the Royal College of Art in London, where I met Brian Eno who gave my confused 'jack-of-all-trade' self – drawing, making digital things, making films, making installations and advertising and stuff – the most valuable advice of my life when I asked him what I was. An artist? A designer? A film maker? He said: 'Who cares?' And I stopped caring about labels and got on with making stuff.

I really got into this digital thing and now I am having a great time with pixels.

I have never stopped drawing and I keep three or four sketchbooks at the same time. I have a sketchbook with me wherever I go. In fact, most of my art is made in a book of some shape or form. I am better at drawing in books.

If I were to describe my work I'd say it's a collection of simple sketches recording what is happening around me. This can be poignant or mundane, beautiful or ugly. I like doodling in front of the TV, combining two things I like: drawing and trash. Sketching is a way for me to be lazy, helped by my trusted friends: oil pastels, ball pens and cheap felt tips. I am no good at inventing things. My sketchbook party trick is to draw what I see and write what I hear. A funny sound bite can make a drawing unexpected and slightly twisted. Just like me."

ABOVE / Beach-birthday in Walberswick

RIGHT / *I Just Have to Leave It.* Oil pastels and pen on paper, Majorca, June 2007

I JUST HAVE
TO LEAVE
IT

I LOVE
THAT
PICTURE

BELOW / *It's Been Really Mad.*
Oil pastels and pen on paper,
Saxmundham, April 2006

TOP ROW / *10,000 DVD Players to Give Away (John McCririck).* Oil pastels and pen on paper, Kentish Town, January 2005; *Catmonroe.* Carbon paper, felt tip ball pen on paper, Holloway, August 2000

BOTTOM ROW / *Most Places Will Have a Mild Night (Kate).* Felt tip on paper, Holloway, February 2005; *Bill Oddie With a Wig (Britain's Rarest Creatures).* Oil pastels and pen on paper, Kentish Town, January 2005

BELOW / *Formentor.* Oil pastels and pen on paper, Majorca, June 2007

RIGHT / *Kato.* Felt tip on paper, Holloway, 2001

JOHN HENDRIX

John Hendrix was born in St Louis, Missouri, and began drawing at a young age. After attending The School of Visual Arts in New York, he stayed on in New York to teach at the Parsons School of Design, also working at the New York Times *for several years as Assistant Art Director of the Op-Ed page. John's work has appeared in such publications as the* New Yorker, Sports Illustrated, Rolling Stone *and* Esquire, *among many others. He has also drawn many book covers for the likes of Random House, HarperCollins, Greenwillow Books, Knopf, Penguin and St Martin's Press. He now lives in St Louis with his wife Andrea and son Jack, and teaches undergraduate illustration at the city's Washington University.*

"I have been drawing for as long as I can remember. But I started working in a sketchbook when I was around 10 or 11 years old. I have folders full of comics and Garfield drawings from before then, but it wasn't until I was in sixth grade that I began carrying a sketchbook around with me all the time.

I try not to regulate what goes into the sketchbook. I end up drawing during meetings, at baseball games, in the back of bars during concerts, in church, and especially late at night at my desk when I'm on a deadline for something else.

The sketchbook should be a place where it is safe to make mistakes. If a sketchbook is not a repository of raw ideas, but a touring portfolio of my best work, it loses the very thing that makes it special.

The blessing of making a living doing something you love also comes with an inevitable curse: turning joy into hard work. My sketchbook has always been a faithful reminder of what I love about drawing. In the midst of projects and assignments that are paying the bills, my sketchbook is the vital connection to the joy of making images.

Working as an illustrator, I think it is really valuable to cultivate a love of the process and not just the final product. For me, that starts when I crack the spine of my sketchbook and take the cap off my pen."

RIGHT / "Visual notes taken during a lecture by painter Makoto Fujimura – he was talking about the role of 'monsters' in our lives and our work as artists"

OVERLEAF / *Ballplayers.* Red and blue uniball micro pens, Yankee Stadium, 2004

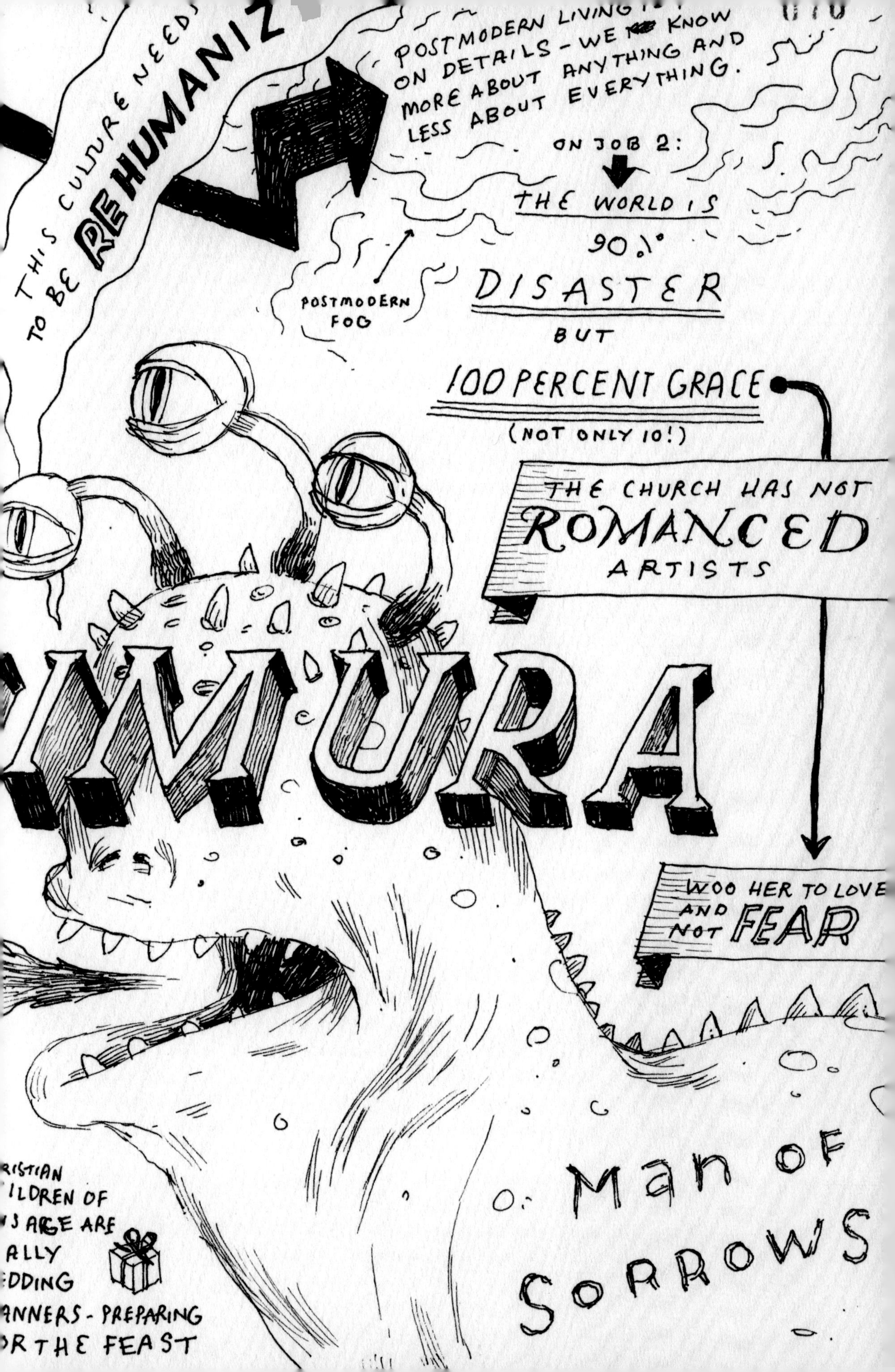

THIS CULTURE NEED[S] TO BE **RE** HUMANIZ[...]

POSTMODERN LIVING [...] ON DETAILS — WE KNOW MORE ABOUT ANYTHING AND LESS ABOUT EVERYTHING.

POSTMODERN FOG

ON JOB 2:

THE WORLD IS 90.1°

DISASTER

BUT

100 PERCENT GRACE

(NOT ONLY 10!)

THE CHURCH HAS NOT **ROMANCED** ARTISTS

[IM]'URA

WOO HER TO LOVE AND NOT **FEAR**

[CH]RISTIAN [CHI]LDREN OF [THI]S AGE ARE [RE]ALLY [WE]DDING [PLA]NNERS — PREPARING [F]OR THE FEAST

MAN OF SORROWS

BELOW / *Jesus Claims "My Yoke is Easy".* Drawing made during a church sermon

BOTTOM / An idea for a wooded installation

RIGHT, TOP TO BOTTOM / Sketch exploring flat graphic and informative drawing; Sketch taken while grounded at airport in Islip, NY; Bird-man sketch taken during a faculty meeting at school

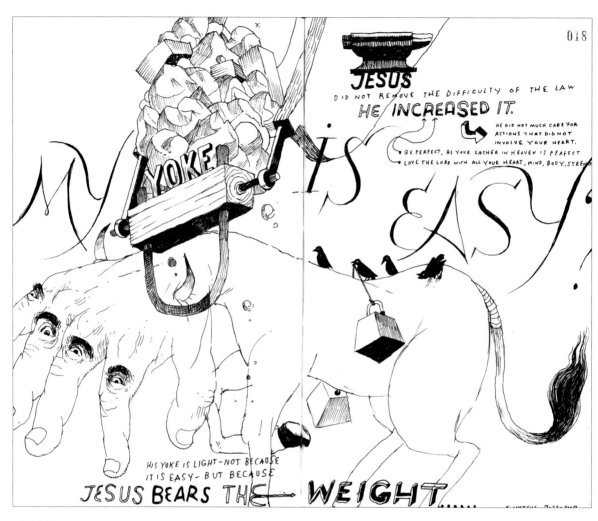

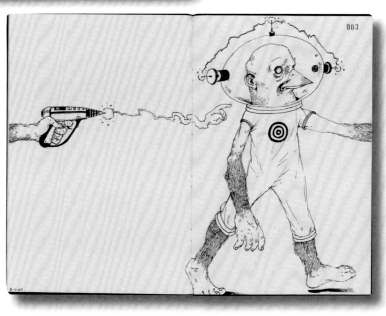

BORIS HOPPEK

Boris Hoppek, born in Germany, lives in Barcelona, Spain. Perhaps best known for his controversial Bimbo Dolls series, Hoppek has adorned the streets of a number of large cities with a wide range of more or less permanent forms and materials. Boris Hoppek & Sancho Panza *was published by Die Gestalten Verlag in 2005.*

"I am resistant to talking about my work, as I am reluctant to explain it. I'm reminded of the time when I had an exhibition – a woman wanted to buy a picture, but her boyfriend explained to her that it was pornographic and misogynistic. In the end she didn't buy it. Some may see my work as pornographic, which is why I don't explain it, but as I see it, there's a little bit of sex everywhere.

I have many sketchbooks – two I'm working on at the moment, another five or six are lying around waiting to be realized. I also have a box of sketchbooks going back 20 years, although when I was young I was less interested in drawing, more interested in the plain paper.

If I get bored drawing beautiful girls, I draw ugly, bad, wild men, or I draw how I will paint my next van. Maybe the next van should be a booty porn club van (lots of naked girls), then perhaps certain people might be afraid to steal it or break into it. I recently had my car broken into and lost everything from my credit cards to my surfboard and, most importantly, my sketchbook.

My sketchbooks are a sort of diary, although I don't draw about myself so much as observe. Whenever I'm bored, I'll go walking around the neighbourhood, talking and looking around. In my neighbourhood it's heavy brainstorming, glue-junkie-brainless kids smashing cars, gypsies, and a grandma who wipes her dog's ass clean. I'll stop at a café and have tea and cake, and sketch and draw. I don't have a real studio, and I don't really need one. Anywhere I am is my studio, that may be a café, or it may be the beach.

I draw mostly in black, but I also use a fat Japanese ball pen with seven colours, some of which are fluorescent. When I think about it I have so many sketchbooks, ideas and sketches lying around the place that I realize that I will never have time to transform them, as I'm always sketching. For me sketchbooks are not just sketchbooks, they are artwork, very simple, raw and reduced."

ABOVE / "Working in my studio on a model for the Exposition 2006 in the south of Spain"

ALL OTHER IMAGES / *Untitled.* Pen on paper, 2006–07

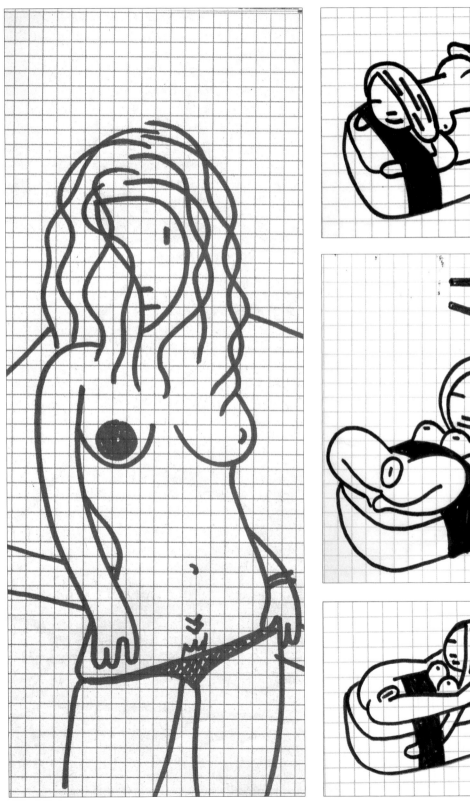

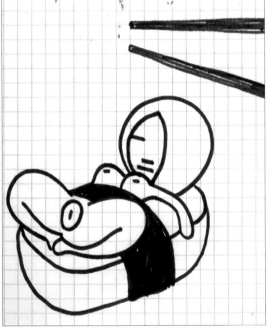

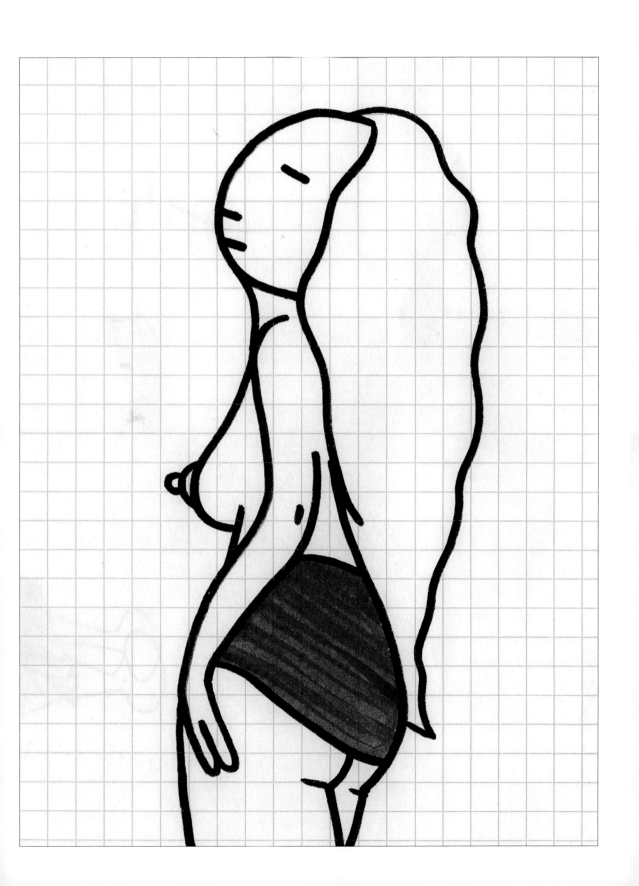

SEB
JARNOT

Seb Jarnot has worked as a freelance illustrator for ten years. His work has appeared in several French magazines and newspapers, including Les Inrocks, Coda *and* Liberation. *The French electronics label F Communications commissioned him to create a series of record covers for artists such as Laurent Garnier, St Germain, Llorca and Manu Le Malin. In 2002, Wieden+Kennedy asked him to create visuals for an international Nike print campaign. His work is often featured in books and magazines such as* sampler2, Graphic, Hand to Eye, Übersee *and* Sonic. *In 2004 Die Gestalten Verlag published Jarnot's own book* 3x7=15. *He lives and works in Nîmes in the south of France.*

"I always listen to music while I draw. I see my drawings as music – they're improvization. I love music with a restrained violence, such as Sonic Youth. I like very long tracks and noise – repetitive, bizarre and experimental music.

I began sketching in 1998 or 1999. I don't remember for sure. It was the beginning of a new style of drawing in my work. After I'd filled one or two sketchbooks, I felt that I'd rediscovered the natural and instinctive way of drawing that I had in my childhood and that I'd lost between the ages of 15 and 30.

My sketchbooks are a totally free area for me. I'm a bit mystic, I often don't remember the exact moment I made the drawings, sometimes I have the impression that they're somebody else's drawings, and that I receive them as messages. I know, it's a bit weird, but it's a significant part of my relationship with my drawings.

I also have a permanent guest in my sketchbooks, my daughter Lou. I love it when her lines get tangled up with mine to the point where we're not even clear who drew what.

There's nothing related to 'real life' in my sketchbook, no reminders or research for commissioned works. I love to draw when I'm on trains, when I'm abroad; my sketches open up new graphic routes for me."

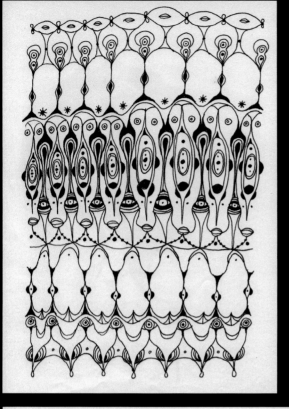

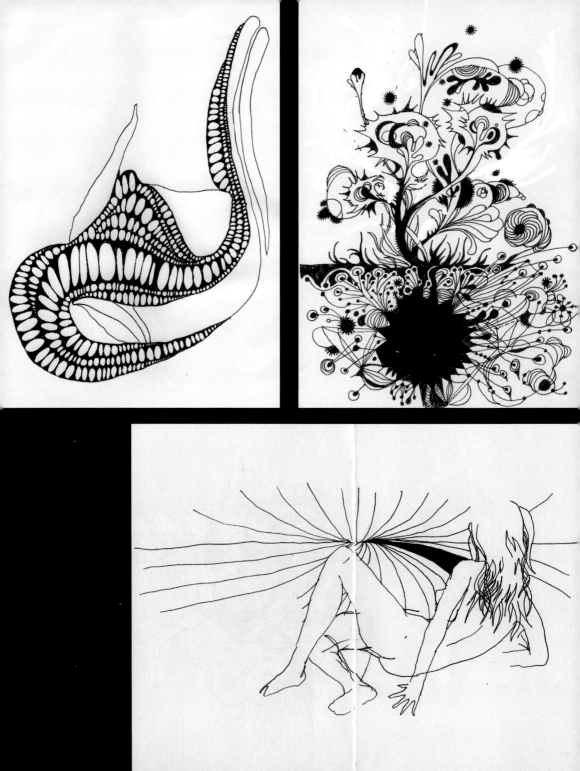

164

Artist and illustrator Oliver Jeffers was born in Port Hedland, Australia. He grew up in Belfast, Northern Ireland, where he began making art and set up an art collective, OAR. His work consists of painting, installation, illustration and picture books, and his clients include Orange, Lavazza, Sony PSP, RCA Records, Starbucks, Candy and the Irish Times. *His picture books are published by HarperCollins UK and Penguin USA. He currently lives and works in New York City.*

"In secondary school I was forced to keep a sketchbook for art, beginning around the age of 12. But at that time it was nothing more than homework. Later I realized the difference between doing something because you're made to and doing something because you want to.

I have kept sketchbooks continuously since I was 18. I think there are around 23 so far. My sketchbooks are mostly paint, ink, paper and concepts that need working out. I have a friend, Mac, who put toast and meat into his sketchbook – they eventually grew maggots.

I like to travel with my sketchbooks; well, at least I'll always have a pen and paper, because there is nothing more frustrating than being caught off-guard with an idea that can't be recorded, or a recommendation of some sort that someone has offered in a pub.

I co-created an artists' collaborative called OAR, with two friends from New York, Mac and Duke, and my brother Rory in Belfast. The first project we worked on together was Book. We FedExed a standard black sketchbook back and forth between Belfast and New York for 36 weeks. Each artist would respond to the preceding double page entry. The order in which we received Book was rotated, and it would be in the hands of one of us from midday every Wednesday to Monday morning, spending the rest of the week in transit. After 36 weeks, the sketchbook had travelled over 60,000 miles. We chose not to discuss the content of the entries during the course of the project, leaving us to interpret, or as it turned out fairly frequently, misinterpret, as we saw fit. When the last spread was finished, before the glue had even dried, we sat around a table in New York, and recorded ourselves asking each other questions regarding what each entry had been about. We included excerpts from this conversation in a publication of Book, and exhibited the project in both Belfast and New York."

RIGHT / *Defeated*. Proposal for an album cover, 2005

OVERLEAF / *Things of Interest*. One of many lists made in 2007; *Easy*. Collage on found advertisement; *Mister*. A study painting from 2006; *Accomplished*. Googly-eye collage

she was extremely ACCOMPLISHED

mister

FUMIE
KAMIJO

Fumie Kamijo was born in Tokyo and moved to London to study illustration at Camberwell College of Art, later being awarded an MA in communication art and design by the Royal College of Art, London. Her work has elements of darkness playing with the surreal. She now lives and works in London, she is a member of Ink Illustration Collective, and is currently working on a project for the Victoria and Albert Museum's new Sackler Centre.

"I don't really remember when I began keeping a sketchbook. I have been drawing since I was kid. I used to love to scribble on textbooks, scrap paper and envelopes, anything I could find. My sketchbooks are a diary, they document my everyday life, my emotions and my experiences. My sketchbooks are about self-confession, they are a mirror and the source of my ideas.

Since moving to London I have accumulated three large boxes of sketchbooks. They are so heavy and take up so much space that I sometimes wonder why I still keep them, but I can't live without my sketchbooks and so they stay.

Everything I have experienced goes into my sketchbooks, the things I have seen, eaten, heard, felt, and, perhaps most importantly, they are the perfect place to document my strange daydreams.

I sometimes think that perhaps I could add some sort of pen holder, as I'm always losing pens and, as a result, always looking for them.

I also like sketching when I travel. I get inspiration from new and different environments, such as buildings, people and nature. My sketchbooks tell others all about myself – they are a glimpse into real and hidden parts of me."

BELOW / *Smoking*. Pen, ink and digital print, 2007

BOTTOM / *Untitled*. Pen and ink, 2006

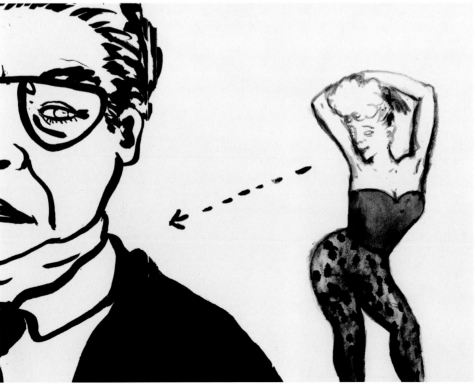

BELOW LEFT & RIGHT / *Bath Time.* Coloured pencil and ink, 2007; *Woman With a Mask.* Pen, ink and digital print, 2007

BOTTOM / *Am I Sexy?* Pen and ink, 2006

OVERLEAF / *Rabbit's Family Tree.* Pen and ink, 2007

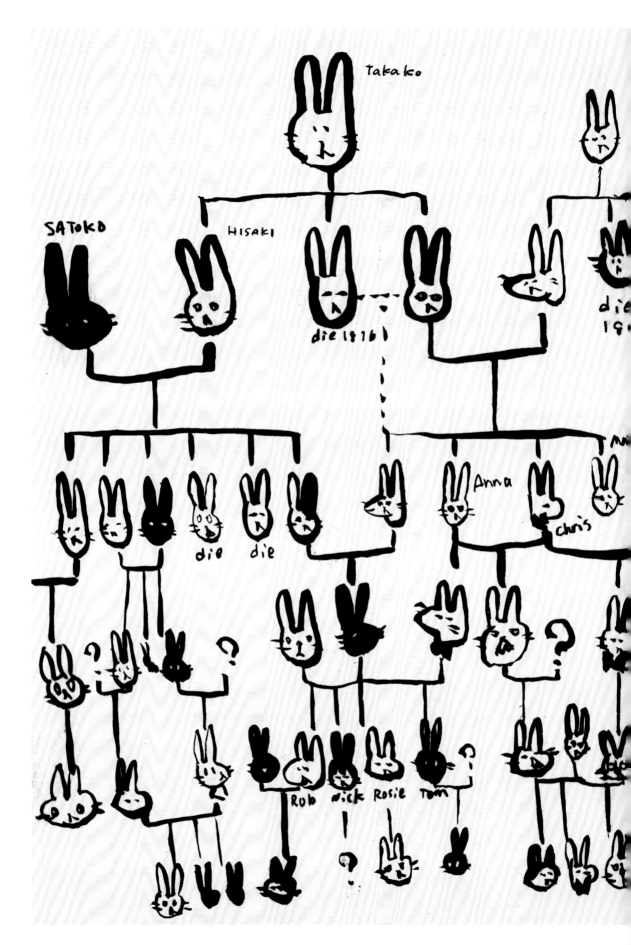

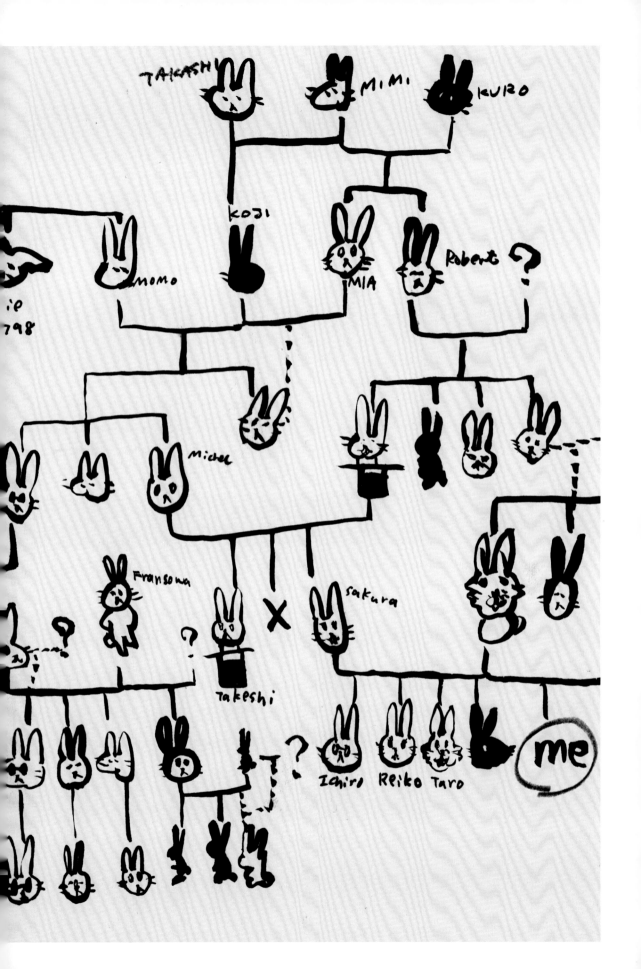

HIROSHI KARIYA

Hiroshi Kariya began working as an artist, illustrator and graphic designer in Tokyo. He later moved to London to study graphic design at Central Saint Martins College of Art & Design, where he developed a particular interest in drawing. Kariya completed his MA at the Royal College of Art and currently lives and works in London as a freelance illustrator.

"I began keeping a sketchbook on my foundation course. My personal tutor taught me how important keeping a sketchbook is to the creative process. Since then I have tried to keep notes of all my thoughts, both in writing and sketches, as a way to document what I see and what I think is interesting.

Just as some people go to the gym every day, I like to sketch; it's one of the ways I find my authenticity. When studying at the Royal College of Art my gym became the Victoria and Albert Museum and the Museum of Childhood, where I would go every day to sketch. I have just started teaching illustration and I have also taken my students to the Museum of Childhood to sketch.

For me sketching is addictive. I take my sketchbooks everywhere, on the bus, on the tube – it's a way for me to chill out, the same way some people would read a book. Sometimes people ask me to show them my sketchbook, but I usually say no and ignore them when they speak to me.

I used to mix writing and images together, but since I started sketching objects and sculptures at the Victoria and Albert Museum, my sketches have become more objective than my writing.

People can see the process of creation in my sketchbooks, and I think they can also see hints of my personality, as they reveal a certain truth, a glimpse of my mind."

ALL IMAGES / Sketches at the Victoria and Albert Museum, 2006

HERCULES
(1617-1697)
BROWN
STONE

ADORAITION OF THE
MAGI AND THE HOLY
KINSHIP, TYROLER
ABOUT 1520

·AVE·MARIA·GRATIA·

RICHARD
COCKLE
LUCAS
1800-83
LADY
CATHERINE
STEPHEY
AS
CLEOPATRA
ABOUT
1836

DAVID d'ANGERS 1788-1856
BUST OF LADY MORGAN

MICHEL-JEAN
SEDAINE
1719-97

AN UNKNOWN MAN 1786

HELMET FROM A SUIT OF GREENWICH ARMOUR
ABOUT 1590

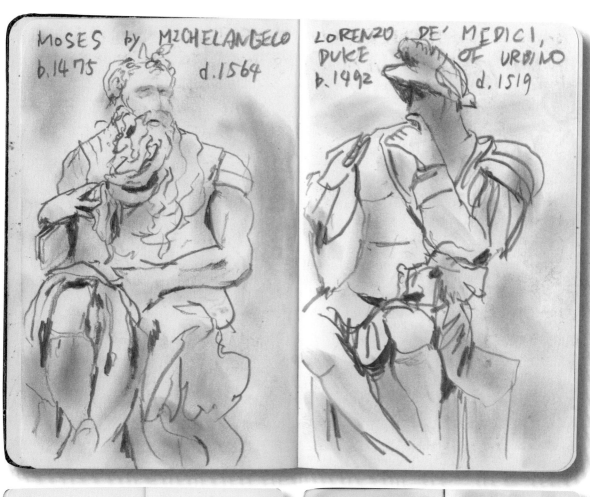

MOSES by MICHELANGELO
b.1475   d.1564

LORENZO DE' MEDICI,
DUKE   OF URBINO
b.1492   d.1519

178

DANIEL KLUGE

Daniel Kluge grew up in Munich, Germany. He studied graphic design at the Fachhochschule, Augsburg, the Istituto Superiore per le Industrie Artistiche (ISIA) in Urbino, Italy, and later completed an MA in communication art and design at the Royal College of Art, London. He has also pursued a growing interest in live-performed video graphics and visualized music. Since 2002 he has lived and worked as a freelance graphic designer in Munich where his clients include the Bavarian Broadcasting Company, Intermedium Records, Johnson & Johnson, Quicksilver, Modart, Senator Film and New Media Board. He is also pursuing an interest in live-performed video and sound, supported by CONNECT and the Guildhall School of Music and Drama, London.

"I began keeping a sketchbook when I was at college. Initially they were uninspired scribbles, but after college I began producing presentations as if they were sketches, but all drawn on the computer. As my daily chores on the computer grew, my head started filling with the desire to work with my hands, using pencils and glue, and so I started a sketchbook again. After a few months I had completed a whole sketchbook without realizing even one idea. That prompted me to take some time off to work on my own projects.

A sketchbook is like a valve, a pressure release system. Instead of weighing things up in my head, I give them a place in my sketchbook. Sketches are like embryos, and as soon as they have been realized, they are born and start to live.

My sketchbook is also a diary, a place where I can keep ideas and refer to them later. Sometimes, if I'm struggling with an idea, I can flick through my sketchbooks and re-connect, be inspired by my own ideas.

My sketchbook is not a reflection of the outside world – I do not go to the museum of ancient sculptures and draw statues. Instead my sketchbook is a reflection of my inner world, without complaints, worries or private problems. As long as I carry a bag, I carry a sketchbook. I have found a very beautiful binding system, which means that I can do my own binding at home. I just collect any materials I find, and, at the end of each day, I bind them into my sketchbook.

Day in, day out, my sketchbooks circle my thoughts, my messiness and my neuroses. Anyone flicking through them would not usually understand anything they find."

RIGHT / *Suitcase 1 & 2.* "Based on the idea of an old distressed book, touched by many hands, these sketches examine the same idea if it were a website"

9 Objekte

Animation

LIVE · IN · BAYERN · 2·R·D·IO · AUS · DER · AKADEMIE · DER · KÜNSTE,

```
decoration:none; color:#0099FF;} #skyDiv {position:absolute; left:0; top:0; width:100%; height:20; z-index:10
9FF; visibility:hidden;} #waterDiv {position:absolute; left:0; top:0; width:100%; height:110; z-index:10
9FF; visibility:hidden;} #popDiv {position:absolute; left:20; top:12; width:103; height:15; z-index:1000
idden;} #picsDiv {position:absolute; left:19; top:3; width:9; height:9; z-index:1004; clip:rect(0,9,9,0);
n:absolute; left:32; top:2; width:250; z-index:1004 ...10pt Arial, Helvetica, sans-serif;} input {fo
```

Piktos
Logos   Privat-Home   Logos.tif
Texte   Service   Text 28.04.99
                                    Katharina Franck
VHV-IhrPartner   Text-layout 1   owerPC
VHV_archiv   roschür

```
decoration:none; color:#0099FF;} #skyDiv {position:absolute; left:0; top:0; width:100%; height:20;
9FF; visibility:hidden;} #waterDiv {position:absolute; left:0; top:0; width:100%; height:110; z-index:0
9FF; visibility:hidden;} #popDiv {position:absolute; left:20; top:12; width:103; height:15; z-index:1000
idden;} #picsDiv {position:absolute; left:19; top:3; width:9; height:9; z-index:1004; clip:rect(0,9,9,0);
n:absolute; left:32; top:2; width:250; z-index:1004 ...10pt Arial, Helvetica, sans-serif;} input {fo
```

Aufräumen

MacApp© ©1985-1993 Apple Computer fruitiger/Arial

Nr.			
B-990407			
Rat & Tat 990406			
Schriftgrössen Manual			
04-990406			
Vhv-Ihr Partner			
Rat und Tat/hell			
Rat und Tat	16,2 MB	Adobe Photoshop© D...	Die, 6. Apr. 199
B-990401	4,2 MB	QuarkXPress™ 3.3 do...	Don, 1. Apr 1999
Rat &tat	3,2 MB	QuarkXPress™ 3.3 do...	Mit, 31. Mär 199
Menüführung	258	QuarkXPress™ 3.3 do...	Mon, 22. Mär 19

M-990401   4,2

Rat &tat   3,2

Menüführung   2,

BELOW / "A design based on a child's lamp. The lampshade rotates, propelled by the heat of the light bulb"

BOTTOM / "A number tree based on random numbers collected one day from the computer, newspapers, the supermarket and bank statements"

RIGHT / *The Defined & the Infinite.* "A composition-based electric trip recorder developed to record driving speed and geographic position, combined with a map of the solar system"

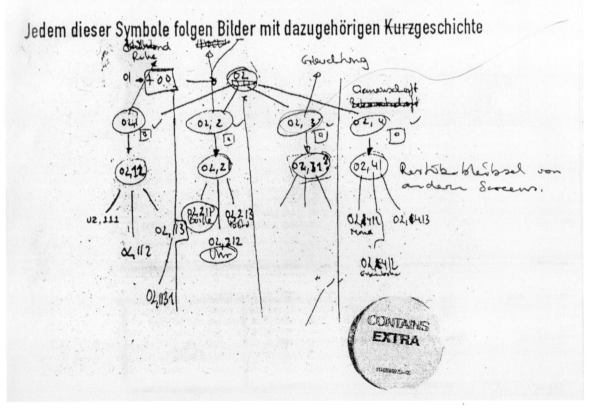

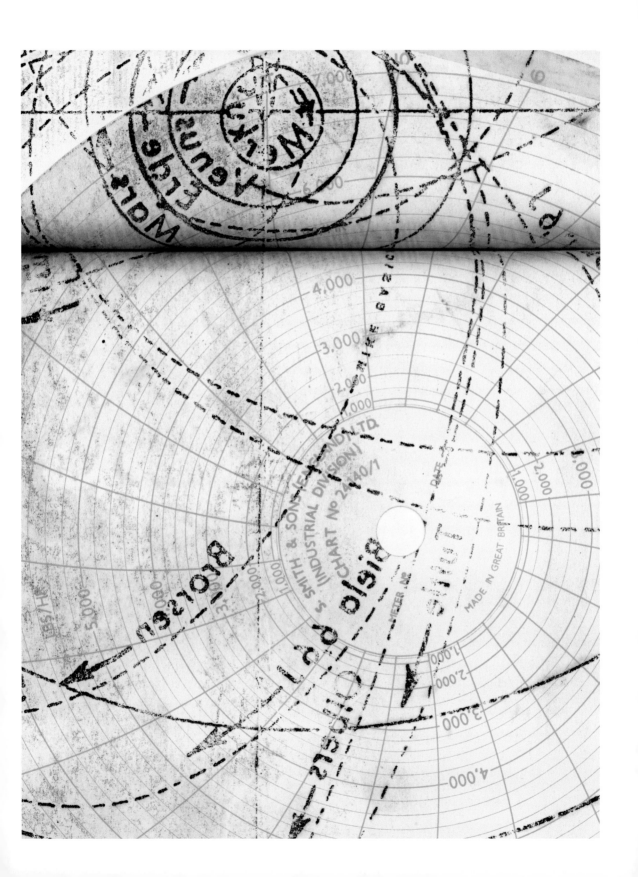

01.11.99

08. September 1999

Puré

03.05.99

WURST

14.01.00 12:06

07/12/99

Eggs

09.10.99 1

Unterlagenschluss

06.09.99

Kas: 002/0010-S
Dat.21.12.1999

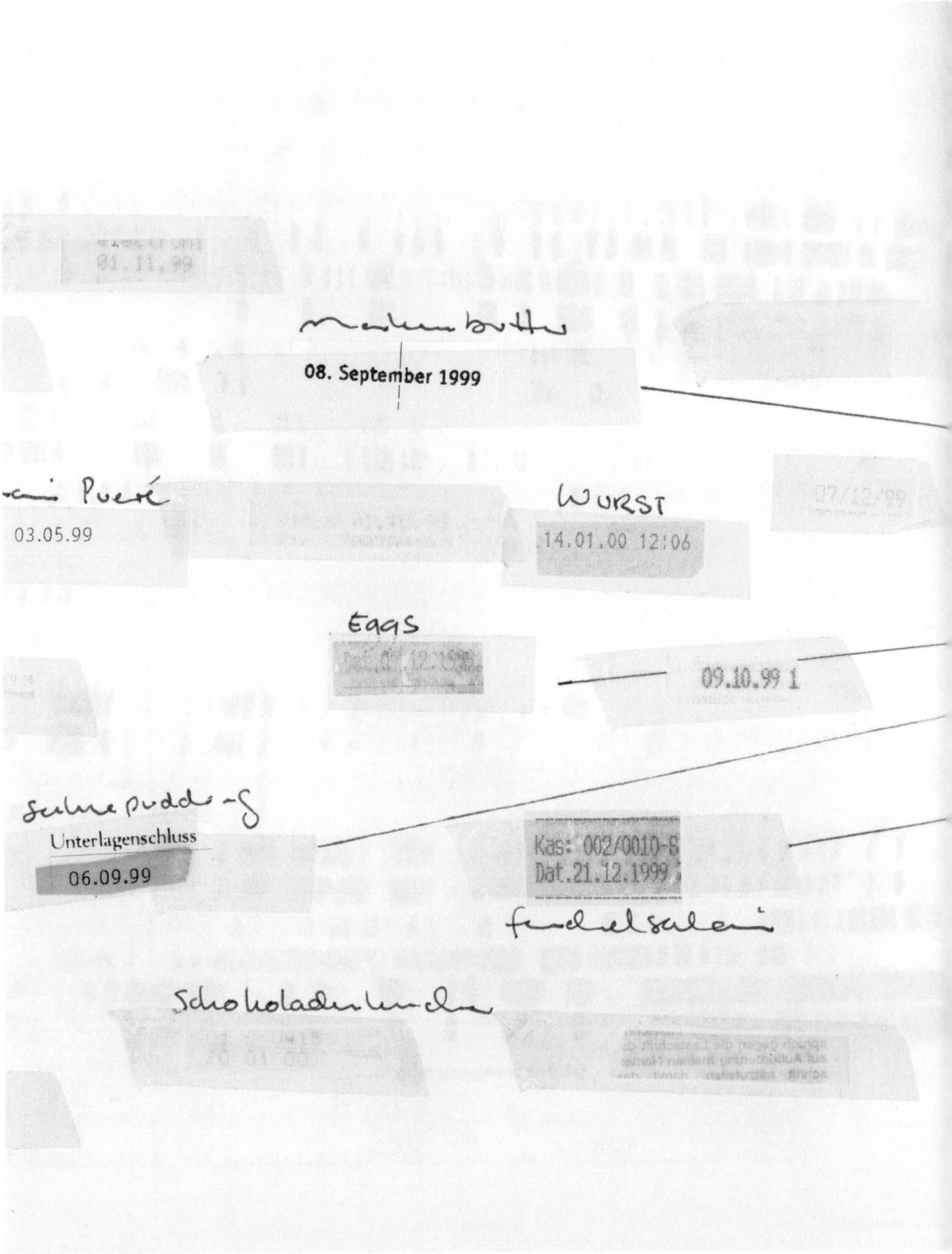

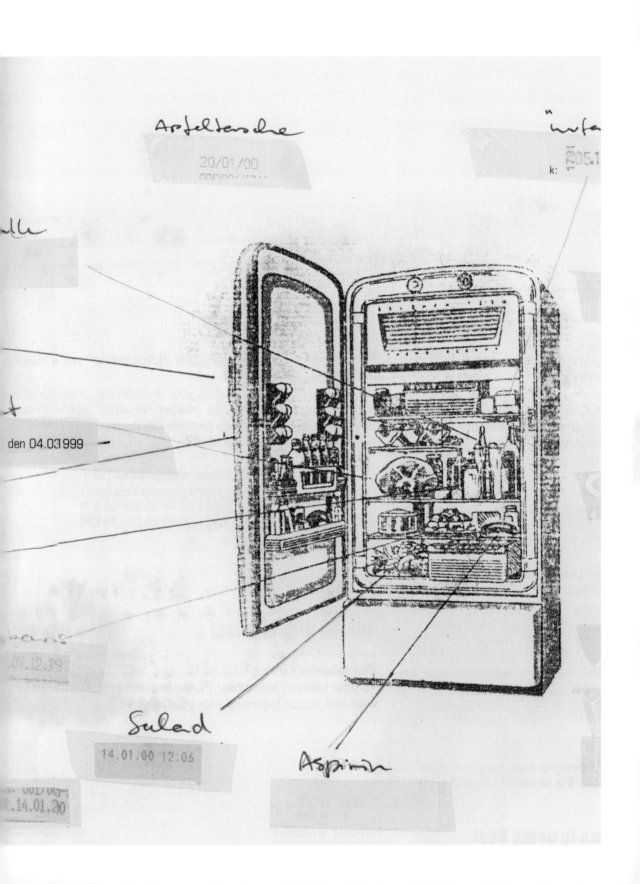

HIRO
KURATA

Hiro Kurata was born in Osaka, Japan, and grew up in Tokyo and Chicago. He studied at Parsons The New School for Design in New York, majoring in illustration. He has worked as an illustrator for several clients, including Tokion Japan, G.A.S. Books and Isthmus, and is now working as an artist. Kurata has shown his work in New York, Tokyo, Paris and Berlin. He currently lives and works in Brooklyn, New York City.

"I spent my childhood going back and forth between the US and Japan. My work is bicultural, influenced by ancient Japanese art, including the Ukiyo-e, Manga comic books, baseball cards, street art and posters and, of course, nature.

I don't quite remember why I started getting into the habit of scribbling in a sketchbook, but it began in high school. Some would make tree houses, I would draw.

I try to draw or write something in my sketchbook once a day, so I guess my sketchbook is also a diary. It doesn't have to look good or neat as I don't usually show it to people. I like the fact of loosening up and going wild, or even being shy. The main purpose is to be honest with myself, let it all out, whatever I feel and think that day.

It is interesting when you start to realize that your lines are telling you something. When I am fed up or, by contrast, feeling free, my lines are very different. When I feel calm and aware of what's going on around me, the lines I create are calm and confident, the rhythm of my breathing and the stroke of my hand link together.

It is interesting to hang out with graffiti writers, as they are so fast and sneaky about hitting other people's books. I remember on one occasion I left my sketchbook at the house of one of the writers, and when I got it back, it was filled with tags and stickers.

I think I would like to add colour to my sketchbooks – it doesn't happen often. I should remember to carry some coloured pens."

186

パリに来て 2 週間。最初の
1週間は 全てが新しく。Julien
のおかげで 楽しい気持ちの一点張
りだった。2週目からは Berlin にいる
時とは、比べものにならない程 充実しているが、
1日に何回か悩んだりしている。大体、リサの
事が頭から離れない。新しい人をさがすか
彼女を追うか どっちかと仇をつた。時間に
かけフしない事だである。
おと仕事、と女
は、僕の中で
大きく広がっている。した事が出来ない
人なんて、女もついてくるか。やりたい事、
知人等の俱辰が大きく世間ではとりま
がられている。あっ奴が一貫かすぎて
気持ちがでっかい。まず、第一戦に立た
なくては。絵は、僕の生きてる胡中
の 50% を費やしても 何達いげない。
8.15.06

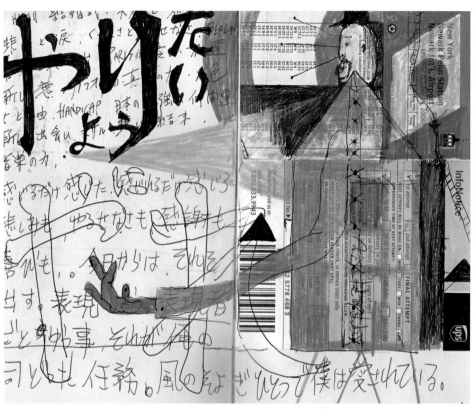

ASAKO MASUNOUCHI

Asako Masunouchi studied illustration at the University of Brighton, England. Her work encompasses illustration, animation and 3D. She is currently based in Japan, working on magazines, books and CD jackets. Her clients include Polydor Records, Le Book, Wallpaper, *Bloomsbury Publishing, Faber & Faber and Random House.*

"I began keeping sketchbooks during my foundation course at Wimbledon School of Art. My sketchbooks are my way of experimenting, a discovery and exploration process that trains my skills and feeds my work.

I have several kinds of sketchbook, one for drawing scenery and people, another for making sketches from books and photos. I like to interpret and reconstruct the images from books and photos from my point of view. Another sketchbook is for compiling collages, and lastly, and perhaps most importantly, there is the sketchbook that I use for struggling with commissioned works – this one naturally is the most chaotic. There is an annual group exhibition at which I show some of my favourite sketches, in frames.

I draw pretty much anything. I don't have rules, but I do avoid dirty themes, and while I constantly draw people, I never ask people to model, as I like to draw them as they are, in their natural environment, unaware that they are being sketched. Drawing people makes me imagine their lives, their situations. I like their dynamic element. Transport, especially flying, also excites me a lot. I love the shape of the planes and all the designed elements of air travel – logos, meal packaging, tickets, etc. It all has a 1970s feel, which I like.

Over a period of time I have amassed a large collection of paper, old paper. My dilemma is that I hesitate to use the paper for my sketchbooks and I find it too beautiful to cut."

RIGHT / *If Only I Could Sing.* Colour pencil on paper and collage, 2004

BELOW / *Sports Sketch.*
Colour pencil on paper, 2004

BOTTOM / *Boy Scout.*
Colour pencil on paper, 2004

BELOW LEFT / *Landmark.*
Colour pencil on paper, 2007

BELOW RIGHT / *A Man With*
Camera. Pencil on paper, 2006

BOTTOM / *Lico is a Helicopter*
Maniac. Pencil on paper, 2002

195

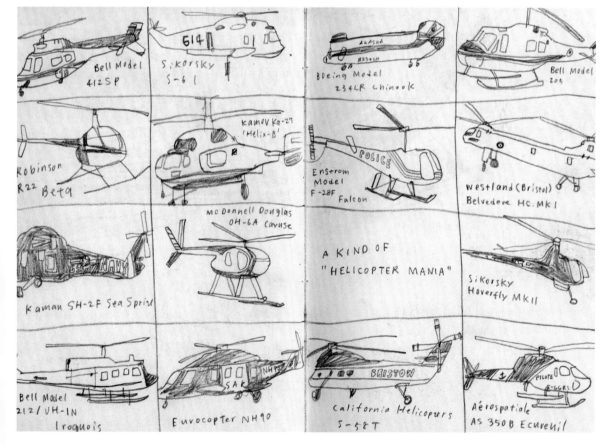

FLAVIO MORAIS

Flavio Morais was born in São Paulo. He worked as an illustrator for a T-shirt company in Brazil, and then studied art and design at the Chelsea School of Art, London. He now lives and works in Barcelona, Spain. His work encompasses editorial, advertising and mural painting. His clients include Once, La Vanguardia, El País, El Mundo, Avui, *Saatchi & Saatchi, Canal+, Spanish TV, Volkswagen and Coca-Cola.*

"I started to keep sketchbooks when I was at art school in London and each year since then I've become more and more submerged in my sketchbooks. Sketchbooks are a sort of therapy, or perhaps even a revenge for all the commissioned work where you're told what to do and how to do it.

For me sketchbooks are a celebration of life and a freedom to experiment. Depending on the particular obsession of the moment, they differ in the length of time they take to complete. My general rule is that anything made with passion or fun goes into my sketchbook, and anything that has to do with control or seriousness stays out.

One of the most important things I seek is spontaneity, and for me travelling is one of the best ways to find it. I feel free when travelling, and that's when I really love keeping sketchbooks. Travelling is a born-again experience, like being a child, and keeping sketchbooks when travelling allows a certain amount of space to express that enthusiasm and freshness, a place for inspiration and freedom."

RIGHT / *La Mar.* Drawing made on a beach near Rio de Janeiro, 2007

BELOW / *Baygun.* Drawing made on an old invoice slip found on the streets of Salvador da Bahia, 2007

BELOW LEFT / *Capcorpeu*, 2007 **BELOW RIGHT /** *Dream.* Daydreaming drawing, 2007 **BOTTOM /** *Trenzinho.* Drawing made while playing with children, 2007

199

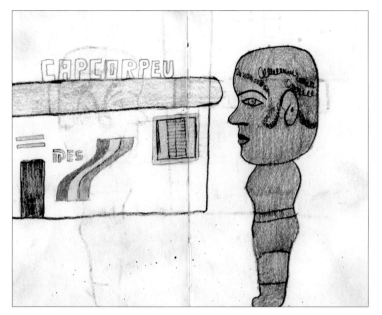

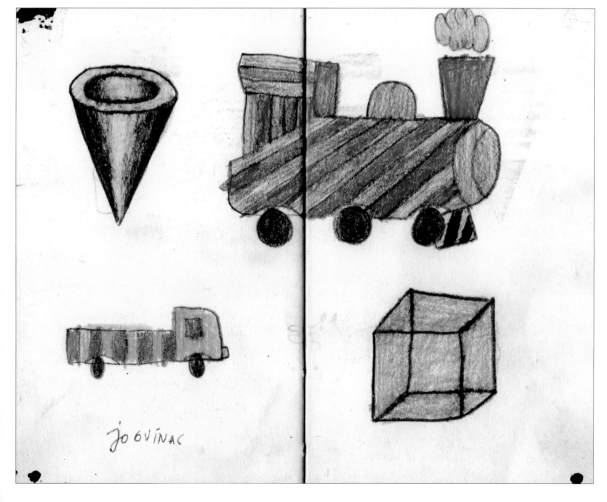

ROBERT NICOL

Robert Nicol was born in Dundee, Scotland. He studied painting at the Glasgow School of Art and then took an MA in communication art and design at the Royal College of Art, London. His ink on paper drawings and paintings often feature recurring themes of men in top hats and images of violence and of a comical sexual nature. He has exhibited in both London and Scotland and currently works as a freelance illustrator in London. His clients include the Idler, Bad Idea *and* World of Interiors.

"The more my life has become focused on the creative process, the more my daily routine has come to involve sketchbooks. I find it relaxing to draw and so I am lucky that part of my day-to-day life involves just that. I like to watch television, and for the last few years most of my sketching has been done in front of it. Some people like to work with the radio on; I like the television, morning, daytime and evening.

Sketchbooks mean relaxation, but they are also work, the jobs I am doing in the most direct way. I think, take thoughts and images from my mind, and give them a physical form on the page.

I've kept sketchbooks for ten years. I know a lot of people tend to write in their sketchbooks, but for some reason I like to keep it visual as far as possible. If things need to be written to help with my process I will usually write on scraps of paper and Post It notes, and then leave the notes on my desk.

There is no image reference (magazine cuttings, etc.) material in my sketchbooks – I keep this on my desk, on my computer or on my studio wall.

I don't always travel with my sketchbooks, but I did take them with me to the Outer Hebrides in the summer of 2007. I prefer to take a camera when travelling – it's good to have a break from drawing when I can.

My sketchbooks are landscapes, faces, shapes, shadows and stories. I am attracted by the good and the bad in life, by the strange as well as the normal."

BELOW / Sketch for book produced by El Bosque, Bogotá, Colombia

BOTTOM / Personal sketch, 2008

PETER SAVILLE

Manchester-born Peter Saville first became well known for his Joy Division and New Order album covers. He has worked closely with the music, fashion and art worlds ever since. His clients include Roxy Music, Pulp and Suede, Christian Dior, Jil Sander, Yohji Yamamoto and Adidas, the Centre Pompidou in Paris, the Barbican Centre and the Whitechapel Gallery, London. He currently lives and works in London.

"I started keeping sketchbooks in my mid-teens so they were mainly pop culture orientated. It was the early 1970s and the first concert I went to was David Bowie supporting Blind Faith, and he was as much about image as about music. My interests became focused through pop, and the relationship between music and imagery.

In the 1980s, as a graphic designer, I was dealing with the visual problems of others alongside my own interests. My drawings showed the visual problem I had to solve, whereas my notes were predominantly discussions with myself.

As my career has moved forward I've increasingly been called upon to diagnose problems rather than find visual solutions, and so my sketchbooks have become almost exclusively notebooks. They include no shopping lists, no layouts, no graphic design solutions – the technical means to an end is not so important to me now. The work one does for others is less personal and rarely emotional or biographical. My notebooks have one subject: What is my work and what is the point of it?

Within the sphere of communication design and graphic design, we do not have a professional vehicle for our own thoughts and proposals. The job involves finding solutions to other people's problems rather than solutions to our own. One of my greatest problems for the last 20 years has been what to do with my own ideas, my notebooks.

I often make lists of words – a dynamic list of 20 words can equal 2,000 words of prose. They act as a catalyst to one's thoughts, a provocation of one another, if you like, notes of notes.

All my notebooks trace my ability to read the world around me, so if I look back through the years, I can see changes in what I notice. When we are younger we see the surface, and as we mature we look beyond it, hopefully with wisdom, or at least more critically. The process of learning to look can make the simplest things quite amazing and beautiful.

What I appreciate about our current cultural pluralism is that it marks the end of the tyranny of particular styles and fashions. It is invigorating to be free to find inspiration in all manner of things around you.

Today I'm happy looking out the window. I see 1960s social housing, a crisis interplay between architectural thought and the human experience. It's a constant performance. If you accept the dystopian aesthetic, nothing is the way it's supposed to be, and thank God. Utopian ideals leave you forever chasing the impossible."

RIGHT / Pencil on paper sketch, 1982

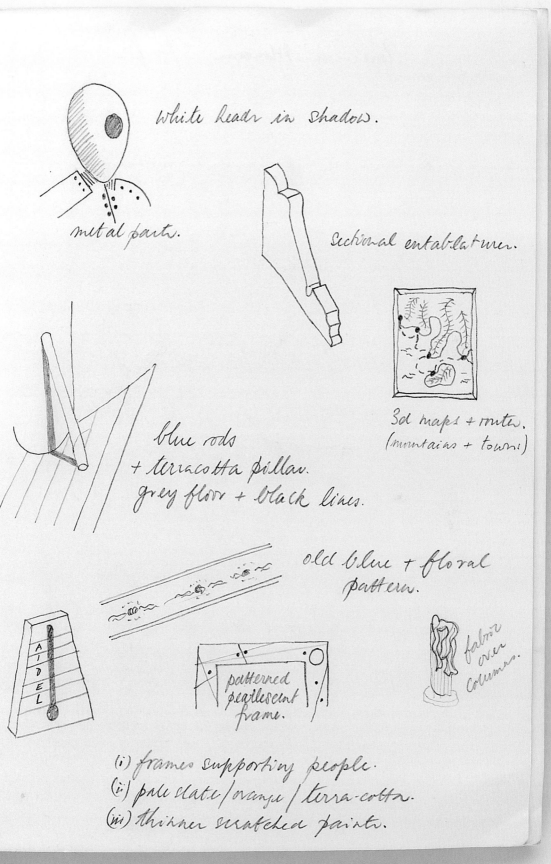

white heads in shadow.

metal parts.

Sectional entablatures.

blue rods
+ terracotta pillar.
grey floor + black lines.

3d maps + routes.
(mountains + towns)

old blue + floral
pattern.

A
I
D
E
L

patterned
pearlescent
frame.

fabric
over
columns.

(i) frames supporting people.
(ii) pale slate / orange / terra-cotta.
(iii) thinner scratched paint.

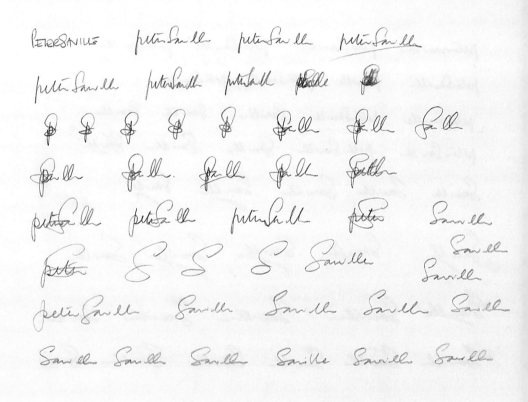

BELOW / Pencil on paper
sketch, 2004

BOTTOM / Pencil on paper
sketch, 1999

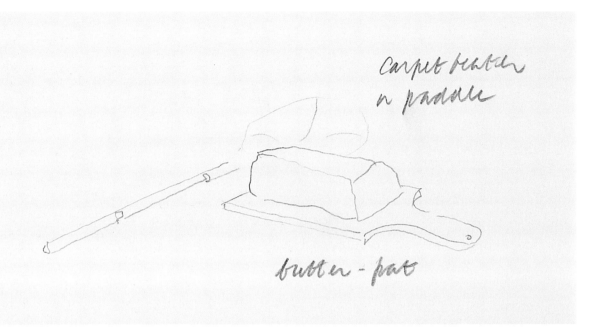

carpet beater
or paddle

butter - pats

20. 08

popular   *pop-u-l'art*

populart   *populart*

liberation   *freedom*

p.l.a   *popular / liberation / art*

people's liberation

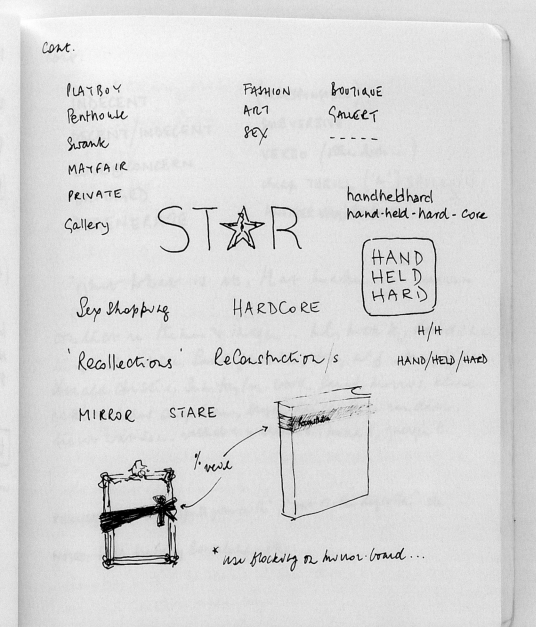

Cont.

PLAYBOY   FASHION   BOUTIQUE
Penthouse   ART   GALLERT
Swank   SEX   - - - - -
MAYFAIR
PRIVATE   handheldhard
Gallery   ST★R   hand-held-hard-core

HAND HELD HARD

Sex Shopping   HARDCORE   H/H

'Recollections'   ReConstruction/s   HAND/HELD/HARD

MIRROR   STARE

% view

* use blocking on mirror-board ...

GUSTAVO SOUSA

Gustavo Sousa was born in Itaguaí, a small town near Rio de Janeiro, Brazil. He lived most of his life in São Paulo. He studied fine art at Escola Panamericana de Artes in Brazil and at the same time studied business at Fundação Getúlio Vargas. After his studies he painted, before joining Unilever's marketing department. In 2001 he joined Cliff Freeman and Partners advertising agency in New York. In 2003 he became an art director at Mother advertising agency in London, with clients including Selfridges, Orange, Coca-Cola and Motorola.

"I think my first sketchbooks were my first school textbooks. I used to draw all over them during and after classes.

Sketchbooks are an extension of your brain. I have a really poor memory so I feel the need to write down or draw all my ideas, because I'm afraid of forgetting them. When I leave my sketchbook at home I feel as if I've left my head at home.

Everything goes into my sketchbook, from shopping lists to pictures of my girlfriend, from drawings of random things I find interesting to ideas for work and paintings. I used to split the book in two halves so one could be my 'work' drawings and the other could be just my personal drawings, but it didn't work out because I can't be that organized and those two things (personal life and work) are sometimes too hard to separate.

I have quite a few loose pieces of paper (for the times when I forget to take the sketchbook with me) that I either staple in or put in the back cover pockets.

I would like to be a bit more organized and have better handwriting. Most of the time I just end up drawing something because I know I won't be able to read my own handwriting later or because I've forgotten how to write that word in English (or in Portuguese).

I like to travel with a sketchbook, especially if I'm travelling by myself. I like to look back and see drawings of somewhere I've been – they bring back memories. It's better than taking a picture or filming."

RIGHT / *Untitled*, 2006. "Done in the middle of a very noisy meeting at work"

BELOW LEFT / *Untitled*, 2007. "Black ink over some ad I found in the newspaper"

BELOW RIGHT / *Untitled*, 2007. "Black pen over Rome's City guide. I did that when I went to Rome"

BOTTOM / *Central Park*, 2006

213

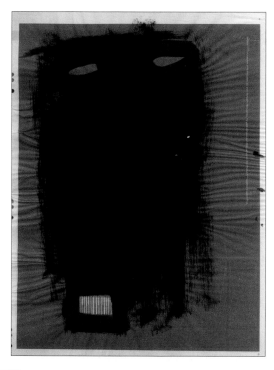

SIMON
SPILSBURY

Simon Spilsbury was born in Somerset, England. He studied at the Cambridge School of Art, then moved to London where he worked as an advertising art director. For the last ten years he has worked across all media, including animation, design and illustration. His clients include the BBC, MTV, Channel 4, the Guardian, *the* Sunday Times, *the* Telegraph, *Nike and Virgin.*

"My dad was an art teacher and so I attended my first art school at the age of four. The penalty for boredom at home, or on a caravan holiday, was observation drawing – matchboxes, glasses, sheep skulls, teasles (every good art teacher had teasles), and so carrying a sketchbook at all times became no less normal than wearing underpants. I don't remember ever having to ask for a sketchbook, they were simply always there.

Sketchbooks are a part of my anatomy. Without a sketchbook I'd feel like I was running naked through a shopping centre. I fill them and then refer to them everyday. I keep one by my bed. Most ideas come to me while I'm walking somewhere and, without a sketchbook in which to document them, all those weird and wonderful things would disappear via the next distraction.

Sketchbooks form the basis of my work and contribute to my social life. They throw up my deepest thoughts in their purest and most spontaneous form and display the brain/eye/hand combination at its most intuitive. I find the honesty of the drawn reaction stimulating and uplifting as well as painful and embarrassing. Less painful though is going back through old books and discovering ideas you didn't recognize as being good at the time, then reviving them for publication.

My sketchbooks are essentially a drawn version of my ideas and experiences. Nothing really stays out of them apart from any writing I do. I like to keep that separate. I don't diarize my life and I don't collect printed ephemera so not many collages appear in my books. Mind you, having recently seen the work of Peter Beard, I feel that I've missed out on something."

RIGHT / *US Male*, 2006. "A sketch exploring the subject of obesity"

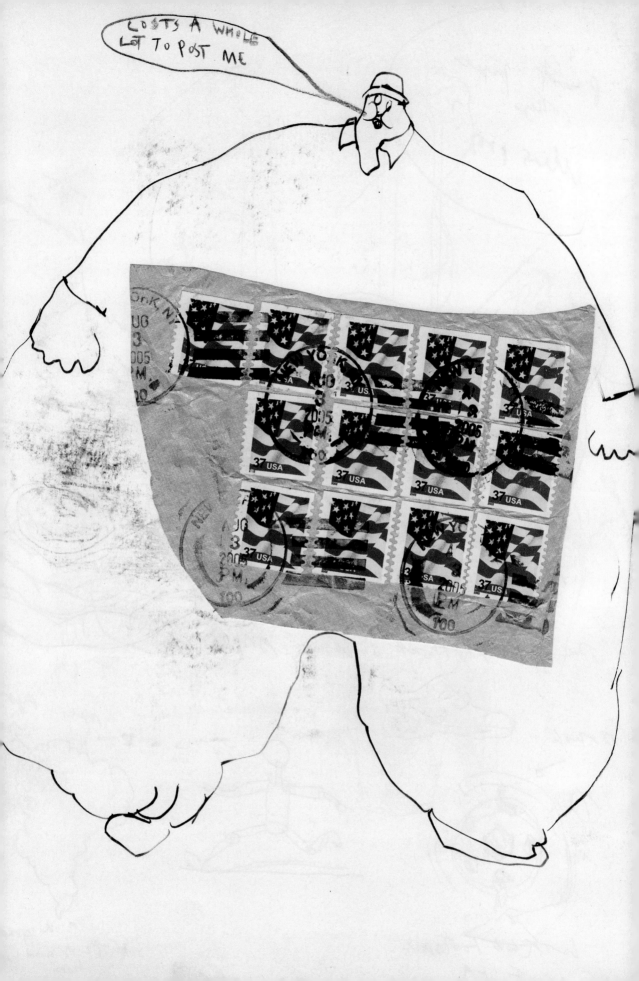

LEFT / *Lifeclass*, 2006

BELOW / *Skeletonne*, 2008.
"Sketch of a skeleton that has
to deal with an obese adult"

217

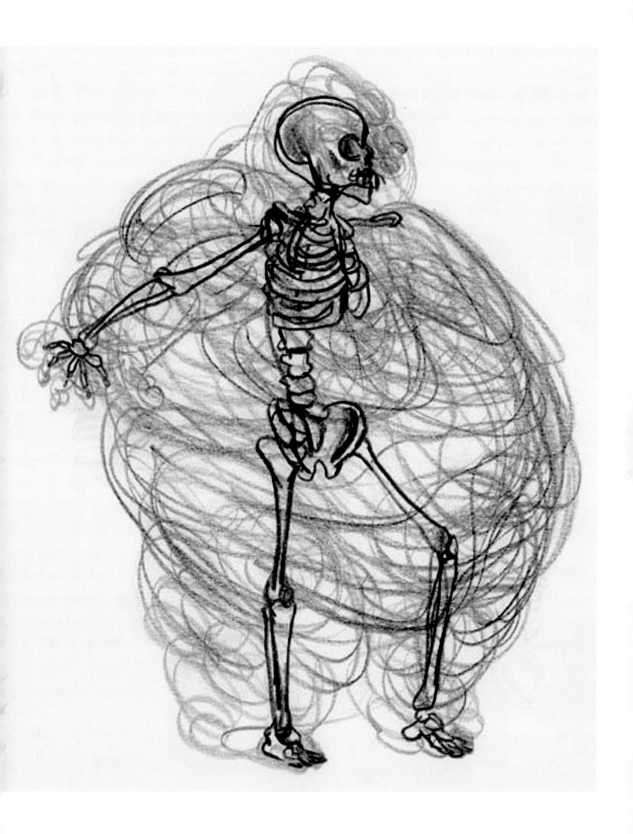

218

Marc Taeger is a Swiss-born artist, graphic designer, freelance illustrator, painter and sculptor, now living and working in Galicia in north-west Spain. He has exhibited his work in fine art galleries in Spain, Portugal, China and Costa Rica, and his work has appeared in many magazines and Spanish newspapers, including El País *and* El Mundo.

"I used to scribble in my books at school, or in diaries. I probably bought my first sketchbook on a trip to somewhere, to have something to scribble down in whenever an idea hit me.

At the beginning sketchbooks were just a necessary tool, but now I find quite a lot of useful stuff in them, even in the old ones. From time to time I go back to look at them, discovering little things I wrote down or drew to remember. And they are quite interesting to look at after some time, because in a way they work like a diary.

I am not trying to make a sketchbook for the sake of a sketchbook. It's a tool. I carry one along with me (usually A6-size) to put things down, to have something ready in which to write down information, whatever. So there is no order, which sometimes makes it quite difficult to find things. And I like adding stuff to old pages, filling out gaps, colouring them in.

I usually buy a sketchbook or notebook when I am travelling. Notebooks are so different in, say, Brazil, China or Japan. But I don't really keep a travel sketchbook. The camera is faster and more faithful to details than I can be and when travelling with people it's difficult for me to keep a sketchbook. When travelling alone I am more serious about sketching things, because it takes some dedication. It is also an ice-breaker, because people are always interested in seeing what you're sketching.

I remember sitting at a table in a tiny bar in Salvador da Bahia, drawing things and people, and suddenly two boys were standing at my side, looking at what I was doing. They also wanted to draw. That was fun. They didn't stop until their mother came and ordered them back on the street to sell peanuts."

ABOVE / Marc at Mogor by Olalla

RIGHT / Four sketchbooks from his box, the top two found in the street, the bottom two from a stationery store

OVERLEAF / *Lección VII.* Page from a grammar book, 2006

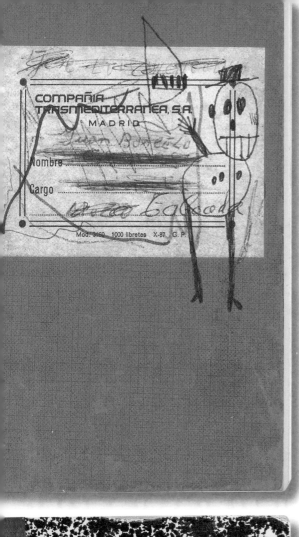

COMPAÑIA
TRASMEDITERRANEA, S.A.
MADRID

Nombre ....
Cargo ....

Mod. 3160   1000 libretas   X-87   G.P.

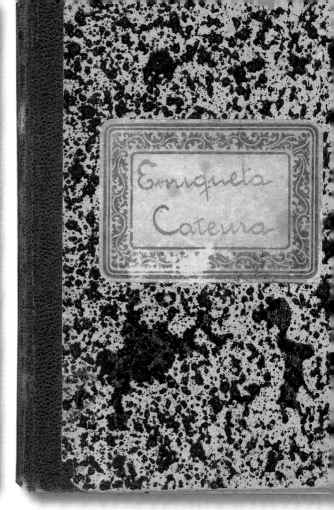

Enriqueta
Caterra

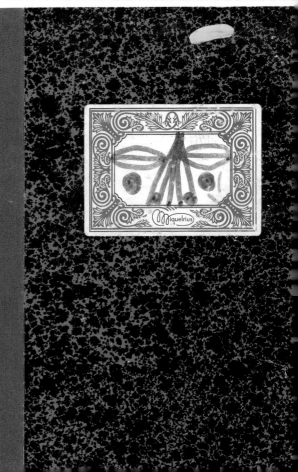

Miquelrius

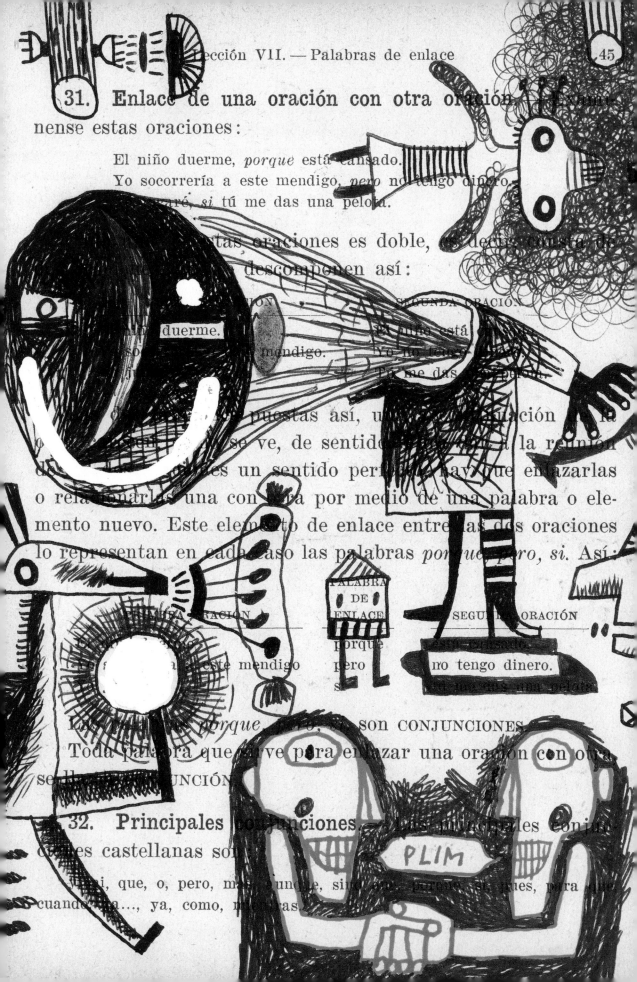

31. Enlace de una oración con otra oración. ... nense estas oraciones:

El niño duerme, *porque* está cansado.
Yo socorrería a este mendigo, *pero* no tengo dinero.
... *si* tú me das una pelota.

...tas oraciones es doble, es decir, consta de ... descomponen así:

PRIMERA ORACIÓN	SEGUNDA ORACIÓN
... duerme.	El niño está ...
... mendigo.	Yo no tengo ...
...	Tú me das ... pelota.

... puestas así, ... se ve, de sentido ... la reunión ... es un sentido ... hay que enlazarlas o relacionarlas una con otra por medio de una palabra o elemento nuevo. Este elemento de enlace entre las dos oraciones lo representan en cada caso las palabras *porque, pero, si*. Así:

PRIMERA ORACIÓN	PALABRA DE ENLACE	SEGUNDA ORACIÓN
...	porque	está cansado.
... este mendigo	pero	no tengo dinero.
...	si	... me das una pelota.

... *porque, pero, si* son CONJUNCIONES.
Toda palabra que sirve para enlazar una oración con otra se llama ... CONJUNCIÓN.

32. Principales conjunciones.—Las principales conjunciones castellanas son:

y, ni, que, o, pero, mas, aunque, sino, ... porque, si, pues, para que, cuando ..., ya, como, mientras ...

PLIM

MARK
TODD

Mark Todd studied at the Art Center College of Design in Pasadena, California and then moved to New York City, working for clients such as Coca-Cola, MTA, MTV, the New Yorker, Rolling Stone *and Sony Music. He has produced many books, including* Whatcha Mean, What's a Zine?, *published by Houghton Mifflin publishers, and* Bad Asses, *published by Blue Q. He now lives in southern California with his wife and daughter and teaches at the Art Center College of Design.*

"Like many kids in the US I grew up on a steady diet of comic books, horror movies and bad heavy metal hair bands. Only I grew up in Las Vegas, and that cranks it up a notch. Las Vegas is strange city, full of Elvis impersonators, high rollers, down-and-out deadbeats, all sharing a surreal backdrop of circus and Roman-themed casinos.

I've kept sketchbooks off and on since the sixth grade. My very first included countless copies of my favourite comic characters, unflattering representations of The Fantastic Four, Spiderman and Howard the Duck.

My second was filled with characters of my own imagination, heavily armoured, rat-tailed rockers, overly spiked creatures and seven-foot roller skaters, Wolverine claw-inspired heroes.

And of course there were traits for each character, things like strength, agility, and their weapon of choice. Later sketchbooks consisted of self-portraits, still-lifes and long-winded notes.

In college, my sketchbooks took on a life of their own. One of the books grew so fat that I had to tie a fabric belt around it to close it.

When I moved to New York I found an old schoolbook at a church flea market. I began painting and drawing in it, obliterating certain spreads while reinterpreting and collaborating with the book's illustrator on others. In was great – every day I would come home from the city and fill page upon page with the imagery and thoughts and emotions of the day. One day I showed the book to an art director. Soon after, others were calling the book in to their offices and pitch meetings. I had no idea at the time that many of the pages I had created just as an exercise for myself would later be used by Sony Music and Warner Brothers and for a Goo-Goo Dolls CD single.

Sketchbooks are time capsules. They hold the past. They're full of ideas, half-thoughts and unfinished business. Some drawings in the books are used time and time again."

RIGHT / *We Have a Lot Going for Us.* Ink on found paper, 2005

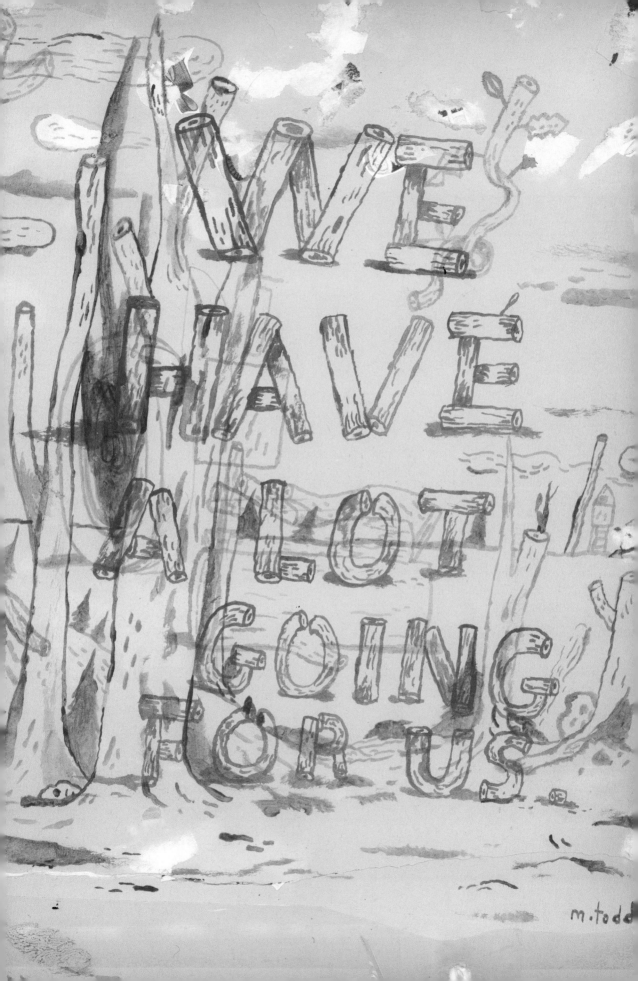

TOP ROW / *Richard.* Ink on paper, 2007; *LA Rap Guy.* Ink on paper, 2006

BOTTOM ROW / *Jeff.* Ink on paper, 2007; *Bin Laden.* Ink on paper, 2008

RIGHT / *It's OK.* Ink on paper, 2006

TOP ROW / *Fate.* Mixed media on found paper (later used as a sketch for a painting); *Tom Jones.* Mixed media on found paper

BOTTOM ROW / *Eyes on Me.* Mixed media on found paper; *Please.* Mixed media on found paper

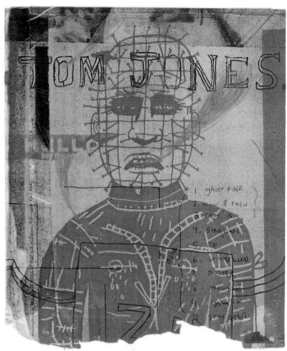

HOLLY
WALES

London-based illustrator and art director Holly Wales is a big believer in self-initiated projects. She is a visiting lecturer at Winchester Art School and has an impressive client list, which includes Eurostar, Nestlé, the New York Times, *the* Guardian, *the* Telegraph *and the* Independent.

"I make objects, draw things, compose pictures, direct projects and always keep a sketchbook. I explore a variety of subjects through self-initiated and commercial work. I ride bikes and use my eyes.

When I am not spending my time gallivanting about the countryside and contradicting myself at will, I systematically experiment with materials and subjects. I enjoy work that has a story to tell.

I am always keen to learn new ways of making things look good, and to have the opportunity to work with brilliant people.

I started keeping a sketchbook eight years ago. I was working on a beach in Scotland and I didn't have anything more than a pencil case. There wasn't a shop in sight that sold art materials, so I made images out of old newspapers – not from photographs but from the typography and the page design. I drew into them a bit, but they were really more about simple configurations of collected stuff – and I took them everywhere. I think keeping a sketchbook is a good way of teaching yourself how to edit well – you begin to fine-tune your ability to know exactly what to keep and what to discard. You realize that what you leave out is as important as what you put in.

My sketchbooks are configurations of shapes, colours and spaces. I collect lots of material from old books in libraries and charity shops and then translate it all through a series of pages in the book to come up with completely new ways of 'engineering' images. I don't see it as collage, because it's not about aspiring to a technique, it's about trying to invent new ones. As an illustrator you'll hit on a way of working that works for you really well – my sketchbook is about making sure I don't just stop there and repeat myself. I am totally against formulas. Or maybe I'm just trying to create so many formulas it looks as though I don't have one – I'm not sure yet."

fofc   rest blown over onto golfcourse

forest blown over onto golfcourse

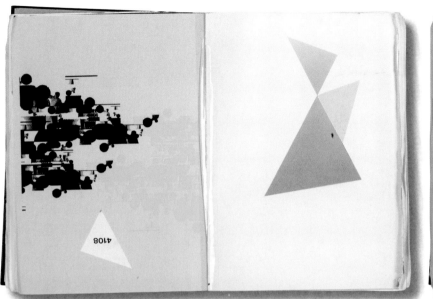

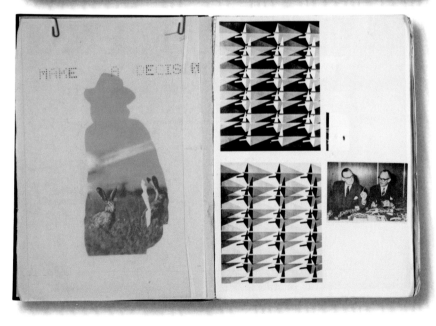

CONTACTS & PICTURE CREDITS

CAROLE AGAËSSE
pp. 10–15
carole.agaesse@free.fr
www.caroleagaesse.com
All photos Carole Agaësse

RENATO ALARCÃO
pp. 16–21
renatoalarcao@terra.com.br
www.renatoalarcao.com.br
All photos Renato Alarcão

PABLO AMARGO
pp. 22–27
amargo@arrakis.es
www.pabloamargo.com
p. 22 Lou;
all other photos Pablo Amargo

CLEMENS BALDERMANN
pp. 28–33
clemens@thepurplehaze.net
www.thepurplehaze.net
All photos Clemens Baldermann

LAUREN SIMKIN BERKE
pp. 34–39
molly@rileyillustration.com
www.simkinberke.com
All photos Lauren Simkin Berke

SERGE BLOCH
pp. 40–45
serge.bloch@verizon.net
www.sergebloch.net
p. 40 Eric Durand;
all other photos Serge Bloch

PEP CARRIÓ
pp. 46–51
pep@carriosanchezlacasta.com
www.carriosanchezlacasta.com
p. 46 David Jiménez;
all other photos Pep Carrió

FRÉDÉRIQUE DAUBAL
pp. 52–55
frederique@daubal.com
www.daubal.com
All photos Frédérique Daubal;
p. 53 20th Century Fox

AGNÈS DECOURCHELLE
pp. 56–61
agneswork@hotmail.fr
www.agnesdecourchelle.com
All photos Agnès Decourchelle

DOMINIC DEL TORTO
pp. 62–65
dom@biganimal.co.uk
www.biganimal.co.uk
p. 62 Dan Wilton;
all other photos Dominic del Torto

HENRIK DELEHAG
pp. 66–71
henrik@benrik.co.uk
www.benrik.co.uk
p. 66 Lana Ivanyukhina;
all other photos Henrik Delehag

MARION DEUCHARS
pp. 72–75
mariondeuchars@lineone.net
www.heartagency.com
p. 72 Tom Harford Thompson;
all other photos Marion Deuchars

ANDREA DEZSÖ
pp. 76–81
andreadezso@gmail.com
www.andreadezso.com
All photos Andrea Dezsö

PAULUS M. DREIBHOLZ
pp. 82–85
paulus@dreibholz.com
www.dreibholz.com
All photos Paulus M. Dreibholz

HENRIK DRESCHER
pp. 90–93
drescher@paradise.net.nz
www.hdrescher.com
All photos Henrik Drescher

JOAKIM DRESCHER
pp. 87–89
drescher@paradise.net.nz
www.hdrescher.com
All photos Joakim Drescher

ED FELLA
pp. 94–101
edfella@aol.com
www.edfella.com
p. 94 Lucy Bates;
all other photos Ed Fella

ISIDRO FERRER
pp. 102–107
isidroferrer@telefonica.net
p. 102 Luis de las Alas;
all other photos Isidro Ferrer

PETER JAMES FIELD
pp. 108–113
peterfield13@hotmail.com
www.peterjamesfield.co.uk
All photos Peter James Field

FUEL
pp. 114–119
fuel@fuel-design.com
www.fuel-design.com
p. 108 Gordon Murray;
all other photos Fuel

ANNA GIERTZ
pp. 120–125
info@annagiertz.se
www.annagiertz.se
p. 120 Ingela Nilsson;
all other photos Anna Giertz

CHRIS GILVAN-CARTWRIGHT
pp. 126–129
chris.gilvan-cartwright@ntlworld.com
www.gilvan.co.uk
p. 126 Karin Mori; all other photos
Chris Gilvan-Cartwright

BRIAN GRIMWOOD
pp. 130–135
brian@briangrimwood.com
www.briangrimwood.com
p. 130 Cecil Holmes;
all other photos Brian Grimwood

JOHNNY HARDSTAFF
pp. 136–141
johnny@johnnyhardstaff.com
www.johnnyhardstaff.com
All photos (including p. 136
'6MM Hate Head') Johnny Hardstaff

FLO HEISS
pp. 142–147
flo.heiss@daredigital.com
www.floheiss.com
p. 142 Kate Heiss;
all other photos Flo Heiss

JOHN HENDRIX
pp. 148–153
mail@johnhendrix.com
www.johnhendrix.com
p. 148 Ryann Cooley, 2005; all other
photos John Hendrix

BORIS HOPPEK
pp. 154–157
boris@borishoppek.de
www.borishoppek.de
p. 154 Patricia Roche;
all other photos Boris Hoppek

SEB JARNOT
pp. 158–163
contact@sebjarnot.com
www.sebjarnot.com
All photos Seb Jarnot

OLIVER JEFFERS
pp. 164–167
oliver@oliverjeffers.com
www.oliverjeffers.com
p. 164 Christopher Heaney;
all other photos David Panley

FUMIE KAMIJO
pp. 168–173
inkillustration@googlemail.com
www.inkillustration.com
All photos Fumie Kamijo

HIROSHI KARIYA
pp. 174–177
info@hiroshikariya.co.uk
www.hiroshikariya.co.uk
All photos Hiroshi Kariya

DANIEL KLUGE
pp. 178–183
kugels@gmx.de
www.danielkluge.com
All photos Daniel Kluge

HIRO KURATA
pp. 184–189
shiloku@googlemail.com
www.shiloku.com
p. 184 Kotaro Tujimoto;
all other photos Hiro Kurata

ASAKO MASUNOUCHI
pp. 190–195
mail@asako-masunouchi.com
www.asako-masunouchi.com
All photos Asako Masunouchi

FLAVIO MORAIS
pp. 196–199
fdemorais@yahoo.es
www.flaviomorais.net
p. 196 Carole Hénaff;
all other photos Flavio Morais

ROBERT NICOL
pp. 200–203
rob@robert-nicol.co.uk
www.robert-nicol.co.uk
All photos Robert Nicol

PETER SAVILLE
pp. 204–209
sam@petersavillestudio.com
www.savilleparriswakefield.com
p. 204 Anna Blessmann; all other
photos PSC Photography Ltd

GUSTAVO SOUSA
pp. 210–213
gustavo@motherlondon.com
www.flickr.com/photos/51659275@
N00/sets/72157594309422852/
All photos Gustavo Sousa

SIMON SPILSBURY
pp. 214–217
simon@spilsbury.co.uk
www.spilsbury.co.uk
p. 214 Richard Chant;
all other photos Simon Spilsbury

MARC TAEGER
pp. 218–223
m@marquski.com
www.marquski.com
p. 218 Olalla Patita;
all other photos Marc Taeger

MARK TODD
pp. 224–229
funchicken@sbcglobal.net
www.marktoddillustration.com
All photos Mark Todd

HOLLY WALES
pp. 230–237
holly@eatjapanesefood.co.uk
www.eatjapanesefood.co.uk
All photos Holly Wales

First published in 2009.
This paperback edition published in 2012 by
Laurence King Publishing Ltd.
361–373 City Road
London EC1V 1LR
United Kingdom
Tel: + 44 20 7841 6900
Fax: + 44 20 7841 6910
e-mail: *enquiries@laurenceking.com*
www.laurenceking.com

Reprinted 2013

A catalogue record for this book is available
from the British Library

ISBN: 978-1-78067-022-5

Designed by Studio8 Design
© Jacket illustration 2012 Sarah Maxey

Printed in China

Thanks to Helen Evans and Melissa Danny at LKP